Leap into LIFESTYLE DISCIPLEMAKING

Take others with you as you follow Christ

MELANIE NEWTON

Melanie Newton is the author of "Graceful Beginnings" books for anyone new to the Bible and "Joyful Walk Bible Studies" for established Christians. Her mission is to help women learn to study the Bible for themselves and to grow their Bible-teaching skills to lead others.

Leap into Lifestyle Disciplemaking follows the pattern of the Navigators ministry for the spelling of disciplemaking and disciplemakers without a hyphen or separated into two words.

This book capitalizes certain pronouns referring to God, Jesus, and the Holy Spirit—He, Him, His, Himself—just to make the reading of the information less confusing.

We pray that you and your group will find *Lifestyle Disciplemaking* to be a resource that God will use to strengthen you in your faith walk with Him.

Christ-Focused • Bible-Rich • Grace-Based

JOYFUL WALK PRESS
Flower Mound, TX

MELANIE NEWTON

Melanie Newton is a Louisiana girl who made the choice to follow Jesus while attending LSU. She and her husband Ron married and moved to Texas for him to attend Dallas Theological Seminary. They stayed in Texas where Ron led a wilderness camping ministry for troubled youth for many years. Ron now helps corporations with their challenging employees and is the author of the top-rated business book, *No Jerks on the Job*.

Melanie jumped into raising three Texas-born children and serving in ministry to women at her church. Through the years, the Lord has given her opportunity to do Bible teaching and to write grace-based Bible studies for women that are now available from her website (melanienewton.com) and on Bible.org. Her *Graceful Beginnings* books are for anyone new to the Bible and her *Joyful Walk Bible Studies* are for maturing Christians.

Melanie loves to help women learn how to study the Bible for themselves. She also encourages women to grow their skills to lead others in Bible study and lifestyle disciplemaking. Her heart's desire is to encourage you to have a joyful relationship with Jesus Christ so you are willing to share that experience with others around you.

Jesus took hold of me in 1972, and I have been on this great adventure ever since. My life is a gift of God, full of blessings in the midst of difficult challenges. The more I have learned and experienced God's absolutely amazing grace, the more I have discovered my faith walk to be a joyful one. I am still seeking that joyful walk every day.

Melanie

OTHER BIBLE STUDIES BY MELANIE NEWTON

Graceful Beginnings books for those new to the Bible:

A Fresh Start (basics for new Christians)
Painting the Portrait of Jesus (I Am's in the Gospel of John)
The God You Can Know (the character of God)
Grace Overflowing (an overview of Paul's 13 letters)
The Walk from Fear to Faith (7 Old Testament women)
Satisfied by His Love (women who knew Jesus)
Seek the Treasure (study of Ephesians)
Pathways to a Joyful Walk (6 pathways to a life filled with joy)

Joyful Walk Bible Studies for growing Christians:

Adorn Yourself with Godliness (1 Timothy and Titus, also in Spanish)
Everyday Women, Ever Faithful God (Old Testament women, also in Spanish)
Connecting Faith to Life on Planet Earth (Genesis 1-11; Revelation)
Graceful Living (the essentials for a grace-based Christian life)
Graceful Living Today (150 Bible-rich, Christ-focused devotions)
Healthy Living (Colossians and Philemon)
Heartbreak to Hope (the Gospel of Mark)
Identity: Sticking to Your Faith in a Pull-Apart World (Ezra thru Malachi)
Knowing Jesus, Knowing Joy (Philippians, also in Spanish)
Live Out His Love (New Testament women)
Perspective (1and 2 Thessalonians)
Profiles of Perseverance (Old Testament men, also in Spanish)
Radical Acts (Acts)
Reboot, Renew, Rejoice (1 and 2 Chronicles)
The God-Dependent Woman (2 Corinthians)
To Be Found Faithful (2 Timothy)

Resources for leading others

Be a Christ-Focused Small Group Leader
Leap into Lifestyle Disciplemaking
Painting the Picture of Jesus (the "I Am's" of Jesus for children)
Teaching Children the God They Can Know (the character of God for children)
Download our catalogue and get resources for your spiritual growth at melanienewton.com.

Contents

Introduction: Casting the Vision for Disciplemaking................... 1

1: The Call to Lifestyle Disciplemaking 5

PHASE ONE: CONNECT WITH NONBELIEVERS 19

2: Build Intentional Relationships with Nonbelievers 21

3: Become a Designated Engager........................... 35

4: Prepare to Share Your Faith Story....................... 45

5: Prepare to Share the Gospel Facts...................... 55

PHASE TWO: ESTABLISH NEW AND YOUNG CHRISTIANS 65

6. Give Believers Strong Roots.............................. 67

7. Choose to Disciple Others................................. 79

8. Nurture Women Who Are New to the Bible 91

PHASE THREE: LAUNCH DISCIPLES TO MAKE MORE DISCIPLES
....101

9. Multiply Impact Beyond Yourself........................ 103

10. Start and Lead a Bible Study Group 113

11. Use Your Workday Lunch Break for Disciplemaking 123

12. Transition to a Disciplemaking-Focused Ministry............. 129

LIFESTYLE DISCIPLEMAKING RESOURCES 139

References 141

Casting the Vision for Disciplemaking

We were visiting a new church. On our second visit, I attended the women's Sunday School class. Several other women who had arrived early were visiting with me and each other. Then, another woman walked into the room and tossed a large binder on the table. "We need to do this," she said with emphasis. Unknown to me, this was the planning meeting for the women's ministry for the coming year. The title of the book was *The Disciplemaking Ministry Guide for Women in Leadership.*

My heart leaped. Only 6 months earlier, I realized I knew a lot about the Bible and Bible studies. But I knew very little about connecting with nonbelievers and teaching new Christians. Back in my college days, when I first began to follow Jesus, I was part of a disciplemaking ministry on campus. I wanted to be part of that again. When I saw that book, I was drawn to find out more. Jesus led me to do that.

So, I contacted the author of the book who happened to be the women's ministry leader for the denomination of the church we were visiting. Disciplemaking was being pushed throughout the denomination, and most districts had someone who was leading the charge for the women in the district churches. I discovered that our district, which included Texas and Oklahoma, did not have a women's disciplemaking leader. So, I applied for the position, was accepted, and began a wonderful journey of training women for disciplemaking in more than 24 churches throughout Texas and Oklahoma over the next three years.

That desire for disciplemaking has continued well beyond my tenure as the women's leader for that association of churches. And my desire to take others with me has not waned. Over the past decade, I have met many women who can relate to my experience of not knowing how to connect with nonbelievers any longer.

GETTING STUCK IN DISCIPLESHIP

It happens over time in large and small Bible studies. Women are excited to study God's Word. As their knowledge accumulates, they often get snippy about the study questions, their assigned group, or the table decorations. I have seen it happen among godly women in very successful Bible studies—women who love Jesus very much. I call it restlessness. We easily get stuck in discipleship and forget our purpose for disciplemaking. I believe that is from Jesus calling us back to our purpose.

Christian women can get stuck in the learning that helps them grow as Jesus followers. They can get comfortable in "community" so much that they lose the drive to reach out to others who do not know Jesus yet or do not know Him well.

Now, do not get me wrong. I love Bible study. I have been involved in some fabulous Bible studies over the years, even writing them and lecturing from my research. Women need to know and understand God's Word so they can know their God better and His way of approaching life.

But Jesus told His disciples in Matthew 28:19-20 to go and "make disciples"—make disciples as He did. His disciples took what they learned from Him and shared it with others, then those could in turn share about Christ with someone else and disciple them. This is the multiplication process Paul described in his second letter to Timothy.

> *And the things you have heard me say in the presence of many witnesses entrust to reliable people who will also be qualified to teach others. (2 Timothy 2:2)*

Transferring what you learn so they can teach others is making disciples who make disciples who make disciples.

WHY DISCIPLEMAKING IS IMPORTANT

I have been in some good Bible teaching churches through the years. A couple have had occasional classes for new believers to get the basics of the faith. But none have offered tools and the push for me to personally disciple a new believer or a Christian who has never been discipled. It seems to be assumed that if someone comes to church or Bible study, they will get what they need to know by just being there. But do they?

When a child begins piano lessons, the teacher explains what the lines and notes on the page of music represent, what sharps and flats are, and which notes are meant for the right and left hands. That is basic music theory. Yet for new believers in Christ, we do not make sure they get the basics in an organized fashion from someone who personally cares about them. And who is modeling for them how to share their faith and disciple someone else?

Enter the "Disciplemaking" movement in evangelical Christianity. At last, something that draws mature Christian women with Bible knowledge like me towards what Jesus had in mind for us all along—intentional living to connect with nonbelievers and personally disciple new and young believers both inside and outside the church. This intentional living becomes part of your daily life— your lifestyle.

Not every Christian woman will become a director, coordinator, or small group leader. But every Christian woman from fifteen to ninety-five can become a disciplemaker. What we all need are the tools and encouragement to do so. I have been gathering the tools to use and am learning how to encourage others to make disciples who make disciples as Jesus did.

If you feel stuck in discipleship as I described earlier, maybe the Lord Jesus is making you restless.

This will be a wonderful adventure as you take the leap into lifestyle disciplemaking. I am so glad to be taking the leap with you.

Melanie Newton

You can listen to my podcasts about Lifestyle Disciplemaking at melanienewton.com/podcasts ("disciplemaking"). You will also find those podcasts on most podcast channels. Search for "Satisfied by Melanie Newton." The podcasts are from Series 17 and have the same titles as the chapters in this book.

The Call to Lifestyle Disciplemaking

JESUS FOLLOWERS BECOME DISCIPLEMAKERS

I t happens over time in large and small churches even among godly women who are excited to study God's Word. As their knowledge accumulates, they often get snippy about the study questions, their assigned group, or the table decorations. I believe Christian women can get stuck in learning that helps them grow as Jesus followers and get comfortable in like-minded community. They lose sight of what Jesus has commissioned us to do—make disciples as He did.

Thankfully, the current disciplemaking movement in evangelical Christianity is drawing mature Christian women with Bible knowledge like me towards what Jesus had in mind for us all along. We are to connect with nonbelievers and personally disciple believers (new and growing) both inside and outside the church. Not every Christian woman will become a director, coordinator, or small group leader. But every Christian woman from fifteen to ninety-five can become a disciplemaker. What we need are the tools and encouragement to do so.

LEAP INTO "LIFESTYLE DISCIPLEMAKING"

Many women like you and I are longing for more direction in our walks of faith than attending a weekly Bible study and the annual Christmas brunch. That longing is a desire put in our hearts by God's Spirit to fulfill the purpose we have while on earth serving the Lord Jesus in our daily lives.

Jesus is calling you! Jesus is calling me! His commission to His followers to make disciples is given to all Christians. Our disciplemaking mission is fulfilled in the everyday world in which each of us will "live and move and have our being" (Acts 17:28). That means disciplemaking should be part of our lifestyle. It helps if our churches give us the training and encouragement to make disciples where we live and work and play. But lifestyle disciplemaking is not dependent on a church program.

As you will see in this book, lifestyle disciplemaking is for individuals. It is something you pursue in your life. You leap into it. To leap into anything requires courage, commitment, and confidence that you will land safely. The same is true for lifestyle disciplemaking.

When you take the leap into lifestyle disciplemaking, you open yourself to the Lord Jesus to join Him on His mission in your everyday life. Jesus is the one calling you to join Him on mission every day. So, He will enable you to do what He asks you to do. And it might even be fun!

Just relax, trust in Him, and leap into an adventure that transforms lives and ministries. We will learn from Him just how we can make "lifestyle disciplemaking" a reality in our own lives.

COMMISSIONED WITH A PURPOSE

Christianity is Christ! Christianity is not a lifestyle or rules of conduct. It is not a society whose members were initiated by the sprinkling or covering of water. Christianity is about Christ and our relationship with Him.

Here is our theme for this *Leap into Lifestyle Disciplemaking* book.

> Jesus Christ calls you to a new life, clothes you with Himself, commissions you with a purpose, and empowers you to fulfill that purpose—to follow Him as His disciple and to live for Him as a disciplemaker.

Let us unpack each of those phrases.

Jesus calls you to a new life

> *We were therefore buried with him through baptism into death in order that, just as Christ was raised from the dead through the glory of the Father, we too may live a new life. (Romans 6:4)*

I love this statement made by a famous Bible teacher from the 1900s. It is the gospel in a nutshell.

> Jesus Christ gave His life for you so He could give His life to you, so He could live His life through you. (Major Ian Thomas, *The Saving Life of Christ*)

Have you accepted Jesus' invitation to give you a new life? By trusting in His death on the cross to pay for your sins, you immediately receive complete forgiveness of sins and this wonderful new life He offers you. You are called to a new life through the gospel.

Jesus clothes you with Himself

With this new life comes a new identity. You are "in Christ." When God looks on you, He sees His son Jesus. By accepting God's gift of salvation, you accept being clothed with Christ.

> *So in Christ Jesus you are all children of God through faith, for all of you who were baptized into Christ have **clothed yourselves with Christ**." (Galatians 3:26-27)*

Being clothed with Christ, you and I are the walking, talking, visible representatives of the invisible God. The gospel message rings out from us like a relay station or a relay runner. See how Paul described it to the Thessalonians.

> *The Lord's message **rang out from you** not only in Macedonia and Achaia—your faith in God has become known everywhere. (1 Thessalonians 1:8)*

The Thessalonians were like relay stations. They not only received the gospel message, but they also sent it farther on its way with increased power and scope. That applies to us too.

Jesus commissions you with a purpose

We actually have a two-fold purpose: (1) to follow Him as His disciple and (2) to live for Him as a disciplemaker.

#1. TO FOLLOW HIM AS HIS DISCIPLE

Jesus continually invited His disciples to "Follow Me."

> *As he walked along, he saw Levi son of Alphaeus sitting at the tax collector's booth. **"Follow me,"** Jesus told him, and Levi got up and followed him. (Mark 2:14)*

> *The next day Jesus decided to leave for Galilee. Finding Philip, he said to him, **"Follow me."** (John 1:43)*

> *Whoever serves me must **follow me**; and where I am, my servant also will be. (John 12:26)*

7

His invitation to follow Him was an invitation to be a disciple. A disciple is an **active** follower or learner. To follow Jesus as His disciple means that you make the choice to learn from Jesus through what is taught in the Bible and apply those teachings to your life, trusting Him to help you do that.

Remember the Thessalonians I referenced earlier? The gospel rang out from them to many others. They were committed disciples of Jesus.

> *And we also thank God continually because, when you* **received the word of God**, *which you heard from us, you* **accepted it** *not as a human word, but* **as it actually is, the word of God,** *which is indeed at work in you who believe. (1 Thessalonians 2:13)*

They were active learners of God's truth and applied what they learned in their own lives. You can do the same. Through obedience to God's Word and humility, you will see Jesus living His life through you and influencing those around you. That influence fits the second part of your purpose.

#2. TO LIVE FOR HIM AS A DISCIPLEMAKER

Jesus' plan all along was for His disciples to become disciplemakers.

> *As Jesus walked beside the Sea of Galilee, he saw Simon and his brother Andrew casting a net into the lake, for they were fishermen. "Come, follow me," Jesus said, "and I will send you out to* **fish for people.***" (Mark 1:16-17)*

Just as they chose where, when, and how to do their work as fishermen, they would also learn from Jesus how to draw people into the gospel net.

> *Therefore go and* **make disciples** *of all nations, baptizing them in the name of the Father and of the Son and of the Holy Spirit, and teaching them to obey everything I have commanded you. And surely I am with you always, to the very end of the age." (Matthew 28:19-20)*

Therefore go and MAKE DISCIPLES. That is the fishing for people Jesus described in Mark 1:16-17.

When Jesus gave that command to His followers to go and make disciples, it was not to ordained preachers, hired church staff, or missionary organizations. Jesus gave that command to average, everyday kind of people like you and I—as we are willing to let Him live His life through us. The commission is for lifestyle disciplemaking not "leave-it-to-the-professionals" disciplemaking.

Jesus commissions us with a purpose. Here is the truth: **Jesus followers become disciplemakers.**

Jesus empowers you to fulfill that purpose

Jesus empowers you for lifestyle disciplemaking.

*But you will **receive power when the Holy Spirit** comes on you; and you will **be my witnesses**... (Acts 1:8)*

*Now to him who is able to do immeasurably more than all we ask or imagine, **according to his power that is at work within us**... (Ephesians 3:20)*

*To this end I strenuously contend with all the energy Christ so **powerfully works in me**. (Colossians 1:29)*

We do not become disciplemakers because we are popular or smart. Disciplemaking is not dependent on being a Christian for a long time or knowing the Bible like a scholar. Jesus makes us able to do what He has called us to do.

You must choose to live dependently on His power by faith. We live by faith in every area of our lives, including disciplemaking. This is what God wants for us. Faith always pleases Him.

*I have been crucified with Christ and I no longer live, but Christ lives in me. **The life I now live in the body, I live by faith in the Son of God,** who loved me and gave himself for me. (Galatians 2:20)*

The Holy Spirit in you gives you everything you need to be a disciplemaker for Jesus as part of your daily life. We are simply to obey Jesus and trust His Spirit to work through us. Can it be scary? Yes. Being scared is a good thing. It makes us rely on Him more. Go ahead and say it right now, "Lord, I can't, but you can in me. I will trust you to make me a disciplemaker for you." Jesus followers become disciplemakers.

DISCIPLESHIP AND DISCIPLEMAKING

Most of us are familiar with the term discipleship. We talk about discipleship in our churches. Discipleship and disciplemaking are NOT the same. Let me explain.

❖ **Discipleship** is the normal process for Christians to get established and grow in their faith—Bible study, classes, sermons, small groups, personal devotions. Discipleship tends to be inward-focused. *Think: Teaching, Learning, Personal growth*

❖ **Disciplemaking** is seeing people trust in Christ and grow in Him while at the same time equipping them to go back and help others repeat this process. Disciplemaking is outward-focused. *Think: Training and Reaching Out, Others' growth*

Discipleship is part of disciplemaking. You trust in Christ, choose to follow and grow in your faith (discipleship) **while at the same time** reach new people for Christ, build them up in the faith, and help them reach their peers (disciplemaking). Discipleship is incomplete without disciplemaking. Jesus did not leave the option open for us to focus only on ourselves (Matthew 28:18-19).

An example that shows the difference

Here is one of my favorite examples to see the difference between discipleship and disciplemaking:

The movie *Julie and Julia* (released 2009) portrays a young woman named Julie Powell who becomes a disciple of Julia Child through her cookbook, *Mastering the Art of French Cooking*.

As a disciple, Julie P studied the recipes and followed the procedures. She experienced the joy of cooking and eating delicious food as Julia C taught her through the book. In a sense, Julie P got to know Julia C "personally" though they never met. That is traditional DISCIPLESHIP.

Julie P did not keep her good cooking to herself. She wrote a blog, taking others along with her. That blog later became a book then the movie. Many women who may never have heard of Julia Child bought her book and started cooking through it because of Julie Powell's influence. That is DISCIPLEMAKING.

While Julie P was following Julia C as her disciple, she was also engaging and introducing others to Julia, sharing what she was learning so they could cook that way too. Julie P was both a follower and a disciplemaker at the same time. Jesus followers become disciplemakers too.

GETTING SIDETRACKED FROM DISCIPLEMAKING

I was part of a campus ministry with a disciplemaking focus while in college. Someone mentored me and showed me how to share my faith with others. After college, I enjoyed community in various churches, did lots of Bible studies, became a Bible study leader, and even trained others to lead Bible studies. Through the years of active church involvement, I lost connection with those who did not know Jesus. This happens so easily to Christians. I wrote about it in my "Overcoming the Holy Huddle Infection" blog post on my website.

Have you been part of a disciplemaking ministry? Or have you heard Matthew 28:18-20 taught so you know you are supposed to make disciples? We know our purpose, but we often get sidetracked from it. Sometimes feelings of inadequacy or fear of rejection will make us hold back and "leave it to the professionals." We also get sidetracked by a lack of training and encouragement for lifestyle disciplemaking.

About 10 years ago, I began to feel a restlessness. I recognized in myself that I was comfortable with growing as a Christian and enjoying community with other believers. I realized that I had been focusing almost entirely on helping women get more Bible knowledge through the years. We were feasting on great food!

Growing believers is very important—essential! Discipleship should have a high priority in our churches and our own lives. But my church did not offer a course for new Christians to get them established in the basics of the Christian faith. Our women's ministry trained workers for leading Bible studies, but we did not get trained for reaching the lost. There was no training for personally discipling new believers. There was no training for us to become disciplemakers in our daily lives. We were encouraged to invite people to church so that they could hear what they needed there.

Jesus commissioned us with a purpose: to follow Him as His disciples while living for Him as disciplemakers. When Jesus commissioned His disciples, they knew what He was asking them to do. They watched Him. Then, they were willing to take that experience to the lost, hurting, and hopeless people they met.

11

Those early disciples were no different as people than we are except they physically beheld the risen Christ. We must see Him through eyes of faith and allow the gospels to leap off the page revealing our Lord. You and I must frequently read the Gospels, tell the stories, and watch movies as often as needed to know His life well because **Christianity is Christ!**

Hooray for the recent disciplemaking movement in evangelical Christianity. At last, there is something that draws mature Christian women with Bible knowledge like you and I have towards what Jesus had in mind for us all along. That is intentional living to connect with nonbelievers and disciple new and growing believers both **inside and outside the local church**. Disciplemaking is intentional and relational.

DISCIPLEMAKING IS INTENTIONAL AND RELATIONAL

Jesus' example in the gospels reveals to us that lifestyle disciplemaking is an **intentional, relational** process flowing from a love for God and love from God for people.

One day, a young lawyer asked Jesus what was the greatest commandment.

> *Jesus replied: "'**Love the Lord your God** with all your heart and with all your soul and with all your mind.' This is the first and greatest commandment. And the second is like it: '**Love your neighbor** as yourself.'" (Matthew 22:37-39)*

Love God first. Out of that comes a love from God for people.

Jesus' recorded ministry spanned about 3 ½ years. His life portrayed in the gospels reveals an overall pattern to His ministry that He modeled to His own disciples. He **connected** with people. He **established** followers in God's truth. And He **launched** His committed followers out in the world to connect with and establish others for Christ.

Jesus was intentional in what He did. To be intentional means to be *deliberate*. That includes doing things on purpose and to be strategic. Jesus was relational in His ministry. To be relational means to be *together*. That includes spending time to listen, talk, know, and be known. We can do that too.

One of our biggest challenges to lifestyle disciplemaking is our experience and what we have seen done. We have become church dependent and pastor dependent to both share the gospel and make sure everyone gets taught truth.

Unless individual members are actually out there making disciples, then you have no disciplemaking going on. The building cannot do it. The website cannot do it. The church value statement cannot do it. Disciplemaking requires individuals to do it. That is what Jesus planned for us. He commissioned all followers to make disciples as part of their daily lifestyle.

As one who has already chosen to follow Jesus as His disciple and grow in Him, you can pursue lifestyle disciplemaking by:

❖ **Connecting with** those who need to know Jesus

❖ **Establishing** new and young believers in the truths of the faith

❖ **Launching growing believers to** connect with and establish their peers for Christ

Those are the three phases of disciplemaking. Phase One is connecting with nonbelievers. Phase Two is establishing new and young believers. Phase Three is launching disciples to make more disciples. We will cover each of these phases in this book.

LEAP INTO LIFESTYLE DISCIPLEMAKING BY FAITH

Jesus is with you every step of the way. You can leap into lifestyle disciplemaking by faith:

- *In your personal life and already-existing church life.* Disciplemaking is a lifestyle, not a program.

- *At any age or stage of life.* Someone around you needs to know Jesus or to know Him better.

- *Along any stage of your Christian growth.* Whether you are just beginning or doing it for years, share what you already know.

- *Because whatever Jesus calls you to do, He empowers you to do* through His Spirit. Say "yes" and leap into disciplemaking with both feet!

13

Not every Christian woman will take on leadership roles at church, but every Christian woman regardless of age can become a disciplemaker. Several years ago, a 92-year-old woman came to a "Leap into Lifestyle Disciplemaking Retreat." She went back to her retirement center and started a small discipleship group with the other women. You are never too old. All you and I need are the tools and encouragement to do so. I have been gathering the tools to use and am learning how to encourage others to make disciples who make disciples as Jesus did. Jesus followers become disciplemakers.

STAY CHRIST-FOCUSED & TAKE THE NEXT STEPS

If you feel stuck in discipleship as I described above, maybe the Lord Jesus Christ is making you restless so you will be drawn to become a disciplemaker too. Throughout this book, I will be sharing resources to help get "unstuck" in discipleship and pursue lifestyle disciplemaking. Trust Him to lead you. Then, watch what He does!

The first leap toward lifestyle disciplemaking is to CONNECT. That is "Phase One of Lifestyle Disciplemaking" and the subject of the next chapter.

Many of the lifestyle disciplemaking activities in this book are interwoven throughout our *Live Out His Love Bible Study* of New Testament women. Consider doing this yourself or with a group.

Let Jesus lead you into lifestyle disciplemaking.
Jesus followers become disciplemakers.

TAKE THE LEAP

Thought questions

1. **You are called to new life.** Have you accepted Jesus' invitation to give you a new life? If not, please do so today and tell someone.

2. **You are clothed with Christ.** God sees Jesus when He looks on you. How does that make you feel?

3. **You are commissioned with a purpose—to follow Jesus as His disciple.** How long have you been a Christian? Have you committed to following Jesus as His disciple?

4. **You are commissioned with a purpose—to live for Him as a disciplemaker.** Have you been part of a disciplemaking ministry? What did you learn that helps you to be a disciplemaker in your life now? What questions or concerns do you have about being a disciplemaker?

5. **You are empowered to fulfill that purpose as you live dependently on Him.** Look at examples of Jesus living in a dependent relationship on God as His Father. Read John 5:19; 6:38; 8:28; and 14:10. How is Jesus modeling for you what it means to live in a dependent relationship with God? In what ways have you become more dependent on the Lord than on yourself?

Action steps for individuals

Here are two illustrations that might help you to see the people around you in a different way.

1. **As your farm:** Joe Aldrich in his book, *Lifestyle Evangelism,* suggests that you consider the nonbelievers around you as your "farm." Jesus used that "farm" image in Matthew 9:37-38 when He talked about harvesting a field that is ripe. Your farm could be your neighborhood, your children's friends and their families, your coworkers, or just one person for now. It is different for every one of us. Ask the Lord to help you identify your farm, then:

   - "Plant seeds": Plan intentional contact with the people in your farm on a regular basis. See Chapter 2 for ideas.

   - "Nurture seedlings": Give special attention to those who respond to you socially. See Chapter 2 for ideas.

   - "Tend patiently": Show Christ's love to them over time. Be their friend so they will not feel like they are your project. Learn their specific needs (loneliness, rejection, lack of purpose, guilt, etc.).

   - "Harvest when ready": Be ready to tell your faith story. Share how the good news of the gospel meets their specific need. See Chapters 4 and 5.

2. **As your personal parish:** Barry D. Jones in his book *Dwell: Life with God for the World* suggests that you think of the places you live (and work) and the people who live there as your own "personal parish." Your parish is the geographical place God has planted you and the people He has called you to love in Jesus'

15

name. The neighbors who live (or work) near you are usually not people you have chosen (you may not like them at all), but they are those who have been given to you and those to whom you have been given. And you thought you were just shopping for your own living space not your personal parish! You can read "Live a Question-Stimulating Life in View of Your Neighbors" blog on Bible.org for ideas.

Action steps for ministry leaders

1. Plan a different kind of retreat or conference for the women in your church this year. Go beyond Bible studies and guest speakers to help your women grow in Christ. That is discipleship, but it is not the end goal. Believers grow best when they take what they are learning and explain it to someone else—when they are transformed from disciples into disciplemakers. Be creative this year and have a "Leap into Lifestyle Disciplemaking Retreat." See the details at melanienewton.com/retreats.

2. Read this book and make note of where to incorporate disciplemaking activities and support in your ministry structure.

Prayer prompts

- Thank God for drawing you to His Son Jesus and for those people and events He placed in your life to influence you to follow Jesus.

- Ask Jesus to teach you how to live dependently on the Holy Spirit's power in your life.

- Ask Jesus to give you His love for people that will lead you to be an intentional, relational disciplemaker.

- Pray for courage and boldness when you feel scared to become a disciplemaker for Him.

What others have done

Billie: "My husband and I like to eat out once a week. We decided we would eat at the same restaurant each week, sitting in the same section, in hopes of building a relationship with the server. Over time, we were able to get to know the waitress and began to talk about spiritual things with her."

Patty: "For my daughter's first birthday, I am going to invite the other children in her day care group to a birthday party. That way, I get to know the moms too. I know some of them are nonbelievers."

Becky: "Some of the ladies in our church have been really working on being intentional. That is our new favorite word! I really see them so excited to get out there. They are not shy. This encourages me to do the same!"

Tina: "Today, our pastor really preached discipling and meeting with people to develop relationships through one-on-one with the lost today. It was especially exciting to hear him say this is not a program with our church but just who Christ calls us to be wherever we are in the workplace, etc. He has consistently taught and encouraged others, especially me, to view a church without walls.it has been very freeing as I share the love of Christ."

Connect with Nonbelievers

CHAPTER 2

Build Intentional Relationships with Nonbelievers

JESUS FOLLOWERS BECOME DISCIPLEMAKERS

D o you know the Bible well but have difficulty interacting with the nonbelievers around you? Do you depend on the church staff to not only reach the community but to also teach each person who comes through the door? If you answered "Yes" to those questions, you are missing part of your purpose as a Christ-follower.

Jesus commissioned all of His followers to make disciples for Him. He demonstrated how to do this while He was on earth. It was part of His lifestyle, and He wants it to be part of our lifestyle too. Now is the time for you to become a Christ-follower not only in your personal walk of faith but also in disciplemaking.

In this chapter, I will share with you what it means to be a disciplemaker and give you helpful tools so that you can live intentionally as a disciplemaker in your daily life.

DISCIPLEMAKING IS A LIFESTYLE, NOT A PROGRAM

Disciplemaking is a ministry lifestyle. It is not a program. It is mirroring what Jesus did with His own followers as He taught them how to connect with those who are not Christians, share the gospel with them, establish new believers in their faith in Christ, and show them how to become disciplemakers too.

Disciplemaking is going beyond personal discipleship. We use the word "discipleship" to refer to the normal process for Christians to get established and grow in their faith (Sunday sermons, Bible studies, classes, and small groups). Disciplemaking is the full process of seeing people come to faith in Christ, grow in Him (discipleship), and then being trained to help others through the same process (disciplemaking).

Christian women who are following Jesus can connect with nonbelievers, personally establish new and young believers both inside and outside the church, and launch them to connect with other nonbelievers and establish new believers. That is making disciples who make disciples who make disciples.

Who can do this? Every woman can become a disciplemaker— teens and college students, senior adults, singles, married, widowed, moms, and empty nesters. Take what you have learned already (discipleship) and take someone else through that process (disciplemaking). Not everyone will become a leader, but every believer can become a disciplemaker and choose a lifestyle of disciplemaking. Jesus showed us how to do this.

JESUS BUILT INTENTIONAL RELATIONSHIPS

Disciplemaking starts with getting to know those around you who are nonbelievers. A nonbeliever is someone who does not know Christ yet! She may want to know Him but does not know how. She may not know enough about Him to want to know Him. But we know God desires her to know His Son.

> *This is good, and pleases* **God our Savior, who wants all people to be saved and to come to a knowledge of the truth.** *For there is one God and one mediator between God and mankind, the man* **Christ Jesus,** *who gave himself as a ransom for all people. This has now been witnessed to at the proper time. (1 Timothy 2:3-6)*

If we look at those around us as women who want to know Jesus but do not know how, we can have compassion and courage for helping at least one to know Him. This will require us to be intentional in how we help her as Jesus was intentional.

I like that word *intentional*. It means to be deliberate, strategic, and doing something on purpose. For years, most of my interactions with nonbelievers were casual. They just happened to be around me. Then, I attended a "Disciplemaking Pathway Training" by Jackie Redmond of ResoundNow. In that presentation, I learned the importance of being intentional and relational with the nonbelievers around me. To be *relational* means to be together—spending time to listen, talk, know, and be known. That is how we connect with them. And that is what Jesus modeled for us.

22

The gospels reveal how Jesus intentionally and relationally reproduced disciplemakers...so that we can do the same. (ResoundNow, *Disciplemaking Pathway Training Guide,* page 1)

Disciplemaking is an intentional, relational process flowing from a love for God and love from God for people. Let us see how Jesus did this.

Jesus intentionally went to those who needed to know Him

Throughout His three and a half years of ministry, Jesus **intentionally** went to places where the people were who needed to know Him. He did not let people keep Him in one community to benefit from His presence.

> *At sunset, the people brought to Jesus all who had various kinds of sickness, and laying his hands on each one, he healed them. ... At daybreak, Jesus went out to a solitary place. The people were looking for him and when they came to where he was,* **they tried to keep him from leaving them.** *But he said,* **"I must proclaim the good news of the kingdom of God to the other towns also, because that is why I was sent."** *And he kept on preaching in the synagogues of Judea. (Luke 4:40-44)*

The situation just referenced occurred in Capernaum after Jesus healed Peter's mother-in-law. Notice what the townspeople wanted to do—keep Him from leaving them. They wanted to have their own community healer. Where is the concern for those in other communities who needed His healing power? Jesus, however, knew that His mission was to go to other towns and "proclaim the good news of the kingdom of God." He knew His purpose.

As I mentioned in Chapter 1, "The Call to Lifestyle Disciplemaking," we can get very cozy and comfortable hanging out with Christians all the time. That is like keeping Jesus to ourselves. We need to resist that temptation and understand that our purpose is the same as His—go to others outside of our community and proclaim the good news of the Gospel.

Jesus built relationships with anyone interested in Him

Jesus built **relationships** with those who were interested, and He was known as a friend of sinners.

> *After this, Jesus went out and saw a tax collector by the name of Levi sitting at his tax booth. "Follow me," Jesus said to him, and Levi got up, left everything and followed him. Then Levi held a great banquet for Jesus at his house, and **a large crowd of tax collectors and others were eating with them.** But the Pharisees and the teachers of the law who belonged to their sect complained to his disciples, "Why do you eat and drink with tax collectors and sinners?" Jesus answered them, "It is not the healthy who need a doctor, but the sick. I have not come to call the righteous, but sinners to repentance."*
> *(Luke 5:27-32)*

Jesus recognized that Levi (aka Matthew) was interested in following Him. Jesus invited Levi. Levi said "Yes!" Then, Levi held a party and invited all his tax collector friends. His life had been changed, and he wanted his friends to meet the reason. What a great excuse to throw a party!

Apparently, he had a house full of coworkers! I always want to ask the question, "What made them want to come?" Tax collectors were known to be greedy and charged the Jewish people far more than what was owed. They were in cahoots with the Romans. All of that made them despised. But no one is beyond the power of the Gospel.

From Luke's gospel, we know that tax collectors had already shown an interest in wanting a new life by going out to hear John the Baptist and get baptized by him (Luke 3:12-13). They were spiritual seekers. What did they have to lose? Nothing! They were already shunned by the "religious" community because of their lifestyle. Maybe not all the tax collectors who came to Levi's house decided to follow Jesus, but enough were interested in listening to Him. If someone was not talking about God's true way of approaching life, how would they otherwise know?

This is what is said about those who responded:

> *All the people, even the tax collectors, **when they heard Jesus' words, acknowledged that God's way was right,** because they had been baptized by John. (Luke 7:29)*

> *Now the tax collectors and sinners **were all gathering around to hear Jesus.** (Luke 15:1)*

To those who wanted to know more about Him, Jesus gave them more teaching. He even used tax collectors in His parables representing those who knew they needed God and were seeking Him though the "religious" people avoided them. Besides Levi, Zacchaeus was also a tax collector who turned his life around when Jesus entered his life. He was hungry for a different kind of life. Jesus met him there in his need (Luke 19:2-8).

Another example of this comes from Jesus' interaction with the woman of Samaria in John 4. After Jesus revealed Himself to her, she went back to her town and told her peers about Jesus. This is what happened next:

> *Then, leaving her water jar, **the woman went back to the town and said to the people, "Come, see** a man who told me everything I ever did. Could this be the Messiah?" They came out of the town and made their way toward him.... Many of the Samaritans from that town believed in him because of the woman's testimony, "He told me everything I ever did." So when the Samaritans came to him, they urged him to stay with them, and he stayed two days. And **because of his words many more became believers.** They said to the woman, "We no longer believe just because of what you said; now we have heard for ourselves, and we know that this man really is the Savior of the world." (John 4:28-30)*

The people were teachable, so Jesus stayed with them for two days and continued teaching them. Many believed.

JESUS INVITED PEOPLE TO JOIN HIM ON HIS MISSION

Jesus invited people to join Him in His mission. For some, that meant they were to travel with Him. For others, they were to go back home and share about Him with their family and neighbors.

In a non-Jewish region on the eastern side of the Sea of Galilee, Jesus healed a severely demonized man. How do you think the healed man responded? The same as you and I would.

> *As Jesus was getting into the boat, the man who had been demon-possessed begged to go with him. Jesus did not let him, but said, **"Go home to your own people and tell them how much the Lord has done for you, and how he has had mercy on you."** So **the man went away and began to tell** in the Decapolis how much Jesus had done for him. And all the people were amazed. (Mark 5:18-20)*

25

Of course, the grateful man wanted to stay close to Jesus and hang out with the other disciples. But Jesus gave him a mission. "Go to those who have not met Me and tell your story so they can know Me too." The healed man obeyed Jesus and told his story not just to one person but to many. "And all the people were amazed."

The evidences of human distress are everywhere around us. Women are in bondage to guilt, fear, destructive behavior, and fatigue due to the burden of responsibilities. Erroneous views of God leave them feeling empty, confused, and without meaning and purpose. Failure in relationships produces a sense of rejection, worthlessness, and extreme loneliness. Jesus Christ's plan to meet that need for every woman is Himself. And He invited you to join Him on that mission.

> *Jesus went through all the towns and villages, **teaching** in their synagogues, **proclaiming** the good news of the kingdom and healing every disease and sickness. When he saw the crowds, **he had compassion on them**, because they were harassed and helpless, like sheep without a shepherd. Then he said to his disciples, "The harvest is plentiful but the workers are few. **Ask the Lord of the harvest, therefore, to send out workers into his harvest field."** (Matthew 9:35-38)*

Do you desire to be a laborer for the harvest? I hope your answer is "Yes!" You and I need to join Jesus in the mission to build intentional relationships with those who do not know Christ or do not know Him well. Jesus' example in the gospels reveals to us that lifestyle disciplemaking is an intentional, relational process flowing from a love for God and **love from God for people**. We will start getting ready for lifestyle disciplemaking with something simple—learning how to love people.

LOVING PEOPLE

God's love for people given to you

Do you love God? Then, you know that He loves people. That is why He came to earth to live as a human and become the sacrifice that makes it possible for us to have an unbroken relationship with the God who loves us dearly. You can read more about this in my blog series, "The Gospel: God's Cure for Our Sin Disease."

Because our God loves people, He calls us to join Him on His mission to reach people who need to know His love. We enter into that mission when we consider what life is really like for those around us who do not know Jesus yet. Throughout this series, we will refer to anyone who has not trusted in Christ yet as a *nonbeliever*. The Bible describes nonbelievers as living in blindness and darkness. Have you thought about what life is like for the nonbelievers around you? Do you even care?

I heard someone say this several years ago. It stunned me.

If we aren't careful, the busyness of life will lead to **intentional blindness.** (Doug Pollack, God Space)

Have you developed some intentional blindness? I know I have. In fact, I was recently ignored while visiting a new group of Christians! Two of the women who are leaders in the group introduced themselves to me then turned away and spent the next five minutes visiting with each other. They left me just sitting alone at the table—a newcomer. Awkward. Intentional blindness. Is that how the nonbelievers in your circle of acquaintances feel?

Who are the nonbelievers in your life?

Who are the nonbelievers in your life? Where do you frequently see them? Start with where you are presently connected: School, gym, sporting events, coffee shop, work, family, neighborhood, retirement center, hair stylist, volunteer activity, book club, community classes, and your children's friends. Some we think are nonbelievers may be believers who have never been established in their faith so their lives look like those of nonbelievers.

Ask Jesus to give you His love for them and to help you understand what they are feeling and needing from Him. Ask Him to make you want to step into their lives as a means of displaying Jesus' love and compassion **to** them. Ask Him to give you a desire to get out of your comfort zone with other Christians and connect with nonbelievers in order to build a relationship. Ask Him to help you go from **having good intentions to being intentional—** deliberate, strategic—at building relationships with nonbelievers.

Invite your close Christian friends to join Jesus on mission with you. Do this together. Where could you and a Christian friend go together to connect with unreached women? Jesus took His friends with Him when reaching those who were outside His group of disciples. You are more likely to commit to lifestyle disciplemaking when you have a partner or two.

PRAY AND LOVE

Where do you begin this lifestyle disciplemaking adventure? I suggest you start with "Pray and Love."

Several years ago, I read a book titled *Pray and Watch* by Neal and Judy Brower. The premise of the book was to intentionally pray for certain nonbelievers in your life and watch what God does to draw them to Him. I liked the basic idea then adapted it to a process that added intentional actions to show love to specific people while you were praying for them. "Pray and Love" simply means you intentionally pray for those with whom you are trying to connect, show love to them, and watch where God might use you in their lives.

> *May the Lord make your love increase and overflow for each other and for everyone else, (1 Thessalonians 3:12)*

Ask the Lord to make your love increase for others around you so that you will want to show the love of Jesus to them.

Remember this truth as you "Pray and Love":

> Evangelism is not about you involving Him in your outreach efforts. It is He involving you in His. Only the Holy Spirit can open the eyes of unbelievers to the truth of the gospel...It is the job of believers to communicate the gospel. It is the job of the Holy Spirit to convert the heart. (David Souther, EvanTell)

Here is the "Pray and Love" process:

1. **Ask Jesus** to bring to mind 1-2 nonbelievers or unchurched women in your life. Consider those whom you frequently see or where you are presently connected. Some we think are unbelievers may be believers who have never been discipled so their lives look like those of unbelievers. Put those names on your *Pray and Love* list. You can download a "Pray and Love Bookmark" from my website for ease of keeping track of the women on your list. See "Lifestyle Disciplemaking Resources" at the end of this book.

2. **Pray for each one** whenever you think about her or see her. John 6:44 says this, "No one can come to me unless the Father who sent me draws them." So you can pray: *"Father, please send the Holy Spirit to work in the heart of __ (her name) __ to*

draw her to Jesus so she will trust in Him." Continue praying that whenever you think about or see that person, envisioning the Holy Spirit working in her life to draw her to Jesus. Remember what drew you to Jesus and what triggered your need for Him.

3. **Ask Jesus** to give you His love and compassion for her and to help you understand what she is feeling and needing from Him. What fills her time? What are her struggles? What concerns her heart? Think about her felt needs. Step into her life to display Jesus' love and compassion to her. Example: *"Lord, compel me to love her well so that I cannot wait to be able to spend time getting to know her."*

4. **Commit** to make the most of any connection you have to build a relationship with her. Think of when and how you might get together with her. Consider what is convenient for her. What could you do together for fun? **Plan** a time to meet with her. Take action with those good intentions you have. Be strategic about developing a relationship with her. Reminder: Do not act shocked by her language or behavior. Love her where she is.

5. **Trust in Jesus** to help you see where the Spirit might use you in her life. Rely on His power to introduce her to Jesus through your relationship with her. Join Him as you watch what He is doing.

Let me put in a word of caution here. Love her even if she never trusts in Christ or if someone else leads her to Christ. Do not let her think she is your project or another "to-do" on your list. She will see right through it and distrust your concern for her. The purpose of praying and loving is to draw them to Jesus. You represent Christ to her. Leave it there. Only God can give us His great love for that woman so that we want to love her well, to build a relationship with her, and to consider it a joy in your life to know her.

Out of 100 [people], one will read the Bible, the other 99 will read the Christian. (Dwight L. Moody)

As she "reads you," she will read God's love for her. Disciplemaking starts with you asking our gracious God to give you His love and compassion for the nonbelievers around you.

This "Pray and Love" process is included in the "Prepare to Share" booklet available on my website. See "Lifestyle Disciplemaking Resources" at the end of this book.

MAKE ROOM IN YOUR LIFE

Like you, I am busy with life that includes my family, my work at home and outside, and my church life. I am learning that if I do not intentionally reach out to one of the women on my "Pray & Love" list and make arrangements to get together with her, weeks go by without any friendship-building really happening. It is not just enough to think about it. I must actively pursue this new lifestyle of intentional friendships with nonbelievers.

I heard Bible teacher Chuck Swindoll say this:

> You must give up your convenience to reach people for Christ. (Chuck Swindoll)

That is so true for me. It is likely true for you as well.

To be a disciplemaker, you must leave some room to get together with your 1 or 2 nonbelievers as often as possible. If your lives already intersect (sport teams, work, story time at the library), determine to sit with her at practice and games, ask her when she could meet you outside of work time, or invite her to lunch after story time. Think strategically in the midst of what you are already doing. Show her that she has value to you and to God. As a friend of mine often says, "Love them until they ask why."

GET OUT OF YOUR COMFORT ZONE

In Luke 14, Jesus was invited to lunch with a bunch of Pharisees and lawyers on a Sabbath day. Deliberately placed in front of Jesus was a sick man. Of course, Jesus healed the man, then proceeded to challenge the listeners' concept of compassion followed by a lesson on outreach. That is what caught my attention:

> *Then Jesus said to his host, "When you give a luncheon or dinner, **do not invite your friends, your brothers or sisters, your relatives, or your rich neighbors**; if you do, they may invite you back and so you will be repaid. But when you give a banquet, **invite the poor, the crippled, the lame, the blind, and you will be blessed**. Although they cannot repay you, you will be repaid at the resurrection of the righteous." (Luke 14:12-14)*

I know Jesus was addressing the religious leaders' pride and lack of compassion. But He was also addressing their comfort. It is just more comfortable to spend time with likeminded people (in our case other Christians) rather than those who are spiritually poor, crippled, lame, and blind. Jesus needs to kick us out of our comfort zone too. How many dinners do we host when we invite the spiritually poor rather than the spiritually rich—personally and in our women's ministry events?

Jesus continually challenges my thinking about this. We who are spiritually rich in Christ just need to do a better job of connecting with those (the spiritually poor) who need to know Him. In order to be a lifestyle disciplemaker, you and I need to commit ourselves first to Jesus as **the sent ones**—sent by Him to our world. It means depending upon Him to make that desire in us so strong that we will **"see" the ones** He wants for us to befriend. It means purposefully giving ourselves (time, love, energy) to them as we live each day and week. That is lifestyle disciplemaking. Who is the one Jesus wants you to befriend this year?

STAY CHRIST-FOCUSED & TAKE THE NEXT STEPS

Disciplemaking is the Lord Jesus Christ's idea and commission to all of His followers. What He calls us to do, He enables us to do through His Spirit at work in us and in the world.

When the Holy Spirit gives you an opportunity to talk to her about Jesus, you need to be ready. We will talk about what you can do to "Prepare to Share" in a future chapter. For now, I will share an easy way to get started connecting with newcomers to your church activities, many of whom are unchurched women who know they have a spiritual need but not sure what to do about it. You can become a designated engager. Read Chapter 3 to find out what that means.

Let Jesus lead you into lifestyle disciplemaking.
Jesus followers become disciplemakers.

TAKE THE LEAP

Thought questions

1. If you were saved as a teen or adult, what was your life like without Jesus? What triggered your need for Him? What did God use to draw you to Himself? That may be how God will use you to reach others.

2. If you trusted in Christ as a child then drifted away from Jesus as an adult, what did God use to draw you back to Him? That

may be how God will use you to reach others with similar experiences.

3. If you trusted in Christ as a child and chose as a teen or young adult to follow Him as a disciple, what kept you faithful? What did God use to keep you drawn to Himself? That will be attractive to someone who wants to know that kind of faithful God.

4. What are some ways that you could intentionally connect with nonbelievers in your everyday life (you personally or with a friend)? Where are you presently connected? Where might you step out to be around them? In what ways must you trust Jesus to help you think differently about your daily or weekly schedule?

Action steps for individuals

1. Identity your "Pray and Love" list. Download our "Prepare to Share" booklet which includes a "Pray and Love" worksheet. You can also get the bookmark as a reminder. Pray 1 Thessalonians 3:12 for yourself—that your love for others will increase. Build a relationship with at least 1 person on the list while praying for God to draw that person to Jesus.

2. Plan an outreach with 2-3 Christian friends. Invite mostly nonbelievers and design it with the nonbeliever in mind. What would make her comfortable? What would peak her interest? Make it dual-purpose, if possible (making gifts to give away, doing something for local missions, etc.). Women are busy and selective. Plan a way to follow up with those who attend.

3. Brainstorm through these sample scenarios. What ideas do you have for each case?

   - **Story time at the library:** Melinda and her Christian friend go to library story time with their preschoolers each week. Melinda notices the other moms who are coming weekly and realizes she could have an outreach here but does not know how. How can Melinda and her friend make this weekly event a connecting time?

   - **Bunco group:** Denise is in a neighborhood Bunco group with several nonbelievers. She realizes she could have an outreach here but does not know how. How can Denise make this event a more intentional connecting time?

   - **Office setting:** Amy works in an office with only 3 other women. She realizes she could have an outreach here but does not know how. How can Amy be more intentional at connecting with her coworkers without taking time from their work to do so?

4. Work through our *Live Out His Love Bible Study* of New Testament women. Lifestyle disciplemaking applications are interwoven throughout the study. Consider doing this yourself or with a group.

Actions steps for ministry leaders

1. Start the next summer with an emphasis on connecting with nonbelievers. Women have more time to reach out to their nonbelieving friends in the summer than during the school year. Families gather around neighborhood pools, local sporting events, picnics, and other children's activities (swim lessons). People are outside walking more. Encourage your church women to look around for those with whom they can sit, talk, walk, and build a relationship over the summer. Then, you might have more women ready to invite to your small groups when fall ministry activities kick up again.

2. Choose our *Live Out His Love Bible Study* of New Testament women for your next Bible study to do. Lifestyle disciplemaking applications are interwoven throuhout the study.

Prayer prompts

✓ Ask Jesus to give you His love for people that will lead you to be an intentional, relational disciplemaker.

✓ Ask Him to give you His love for the nonbelievers around you and to help you understand what they are feeling and needing from Him.

✓ Ask Him to make you want to step into their lives as a means of displaying Jesus' love and compassion **to** them.

✓ Ask Him to help you go from **having good intentions to being intentional** at building a relationship with at least one of them. You can say, *"Lord, compel me to love her well so that I can't wait to be able to spend time getting to know her."*

✓ Ask for courage, love, and whatever else you need from the Lord to be a good news bearer to the woman you just identified in your life.

✓ Pray for God to draw her to Jesus.

What others have done

Linda: "I have been more observant of the people around me wherever I am watching for opportunities. I have also intentionally not filled up my schedule with unnecessary things so there is time for people. I have tried to intentionally connect with my neighbors more."

Karen: "My office building has a great place to walk. I walk regularly with a female coworker who does not know Jesus. What I have found is that she will share with me matters of the heart more readily while we are walking rather than when we are sitting across from each other face-to-face."

Laura: "When you are building relationships with non-Christians, try not to act shocked by their salty language. Expect it and focus on getting to know their hearts and making them welcome in your presence."

Tricia: "We host summer book clubs. The books are not necessarily churchy or even self-help types but are considered to have good morals. The women read the book over a month's time then get together over brunch on a Saturday morning to reflect on what they read. Women who have not participated in anything else at our church are drawn to these summer book gatherings. The book reading has helped me to invite nonbelieving women to join this with me."

Elizabeth: "I realized that I was hanging out with Christians all the time. Being challenged to go to where nonbelievers are, I decided to take a ceramics class at our local community center. So, for the next 6 weeks, I may look like I am there for ceramics, but my real purpose will be to build relationships with the other women in the class." (Elizabeth)

Betty Jo: "I have a coworker who is filthy mouthed and definitely angry with God. I have made it my mission to build a relationship with her and show her Christ's love so she will begin to trust me. It is working as she is definitely softening."

Sherry: "I appreciate so much the emphasis on making good intentions become intentional. Having just moved to a new town and looking for a church where my husband and I can serve, this is a great way to "meet" other women and be praying for them. It opens the door for getting to know someone in a little deeper and a very positive way."

CHAPTER 3

Become a Designated Engager

JESUS FOLLOWERS BECOME DISCIPLEMAKERS

Do you love Jesus, love people, and are openly friendly? Do you attend women's events at your church that draw newcomers? I invite you to become a "designated engager" at church activities where visitors might be present.

What is a designated engager? Keep reading. I will explain what it is and why designated engagers are so important for any women's group or church activity. Being a designated engager is an easy way to get started connecting with nonbelievers as part of lifestyle disciplemaking.

Remember that disciplemaking is the full process of befriending someone who needs to know Jesus, helping her learn to trust in Jesus for her salvation, personally discipling her in the basics of her new faith, and coaching her to do the same with her friends who need to know Jesus. It is being more outward-focused rather than inward-focused on personal growth alone.

Every woman can become a disciplemaker—teens and college students, senior adults, singles, married, widowed, moms, and empty nesters. All that is required is a *heart* to obey Jesus in this area of your life and a *choice* to pursue a **lifestyle of disciplemaking**. Leap into it with both feet and trust the Holy Spirit to lead you to women who need Jesus.

PUTTING YOURSELF IN THE SHOES OF A NEWCOMER

For several years, I was active in the women's ministry at my church. When I attended an event, I knew most women there. I usually had responsibilities at the event or hung out with my friends so I did not really notice the newcomers very much. We had an active welcome team, so I assumed the newcomers would be greeted well. I figured they would jump into the mix and connect on their own as women usually like to do. But then, I became the newcomer! It was a vastly different and eye-opening experience!

As I walked into our new church for the entire first year, all I saw was a sea of faces—none of whom I knew. It was a lonely and isolating feeling because they seemed to know each other. When we were visiting various small groups to consider joining one, I was once again the outsider walking into a room of women who knew each other well but who were all strangers to me. I remember one particular occasion when the other women greeted me then gathered in their group to catch up on each other's lives. Only one woman sat at the table and talked with me, letting me know that she cared I was there. I was so appreciative of her. Though we were not drawn to join that group, I wanted a connection with the one who intentionally made me feel wanted. We had lunch together several times. That felt so good to know someone who wanted to know me.

Now, I have a greater appreciation for how the newcomer feels when she bravely attends a women's Bible Study. She comes because she desperately wants to make friends. She wants to know and be known. She may be new to the area, new to the church, looking for a church, or just seeking something spiritual but not sure what.

The first summer study I attended at our new church, I voluntarily arrived early to station myself near the name tag table. It was not my duty. But I figured that if I helped women find their name tags, I could put a name to a face too. When I sat at the discussion group table, I wrote in my study guide the names of the other women at my table and jotted down whatever they said about themselves. I hoped I would see them again before my memory forgot what they looked like. I sat at a different table every week to meet different women. I desperately wanted to know who some of those faces were that I saw on Sundays! And it worked.

That experience has now motivated me to notice a newcomer at an event and make her feel welcome and wanted. I think of myself as a "designated engager." What is that, and why is it needed?

TURNING YOUR RADAR ON

The word "engage" has several meanings. When a man and woman get engaged, they are "committing themselves" to a contract of marriage at some point in the future. Another definition of engage is "establish a meaningful contact or connection with." My favorite meaning is "to bring things together and cause them to connect." Think Legos. An engager not only makes contact but also creates a solid connection. That is the goal. So how does that fit with women's activities?

You are likely familiar with the term "designated driver." A designated driver knows they are responsible to stay sober and alert so they can safely drive their passengers home. A designated engager intentionally makes contact with a newcomer so she feels welcome and wanted.

In a sense, it is turning your radar on when you walk into a room where newcomers might be present. Consider how radar works to locate airplanes in the sky or vehicles on a roadway. The radar provides an awareness to the operators of what is going on around them. A designated engager does the same thing. I now "turn my radar on" when I walk into a room where newcomers might be present.

During that same summer Bible study that I referenced above, a few women intentionally connected with me. They noticed me and remembered my name. That made me feel wanted and included. I am so grateful for them. Their warmth and interest made me want to come back. They probably did not consider themselves "designated engagers," but by their actions, that is what they were. During the next summer's Bible study, I attended as an unofficial "designated engager" to help any newcomers feel wanted and included.

Here are a few things I have learned about being a designated engager:

❖ Designated engagers **cannot have any other jobs during the event.** You can help set up before an event, which is a good thing so you will know where everything is. But once people start showing up, your role is to "turn your radar on" to recognize that person who is a visitor and connect with her throughout the activity.

❖ Designated engagers **are not the welcome team at the doors**. Greeters have a different role and are very important for first impressions. But designated engagers are **the welcome team inside the room** during the event connecting with individuals who are newcomers. And if the newcomer is attending with a friend, that friend wants you to connect with her guest so she will want to come back.

Even weekly classes need a designated engager for visitors. I mentioned in Chapter 2 that I was ignored while visiting a Sunday morning class. Two of the women who are leaders in the group introduced themselves to me then turned away and spent the next five minutes visiting with each other. They left me just sitting alone at the table—a newcomer. That experience reminded me how important it is to make newcomers feel wanted and to overcome the tendency toward "intentional blindness."

A few weeks later, I attended the women's retreat for that church as a newcomer myself, arriving early so I could look for that woman who came alone. It did not take long to recognize her sitting in the foyer. So, I introduced myself, made sure I knew her name, and spent several minutes talking to her. Throughout the weekend, I greeted her by name whenever I saw her. We both benefited from that connection.

PREPARING TO BECOME A DESIGNATED ENGAGER

You can see how important designated engagers are to any women's event or church ministry function. Do you love Jesus and want others to experience the love of Jesus, also? Do you want to be especially friendly to newcomers during an event so they will feel welcomed and wanted? Then, prepare yourself to become a designated engager whenever you attend an event where newcomers might be present.

AHEAD OF THE EVENT

❖ Start with prayer. Ask Jesus to give you His love for women who do not know Him and boldness to interact with newcomers to your event or group.

❖ Remember how you felt when you were in a strange situation. What would make you feel welcome in a room full of strangers? What would make you more comfortable?

❖ Prepare your contact information to give to the newcomer. Be sure to get hers as well.

❖ Research what your church offers for grief care, divorce counseling, marriage issues, parenting, singleness, cancer, and other common needs. If you have brochures about those, get a few to keep handy when you attend the event.

❖ Be familiar with something you can invite a newcomer to attend in the next month or so—your church meeting times, upcoming women's activities, family activities, etc.

AT THE EVENT

❖ Arrive early to become familiar with how things are set up so you can help a visitor find where she needs to be.

❖ Have no other responsibilities during the event other than focusing on the women who are new. It is okay to help with the setup before the event. But once women start showing up, your focus needs to be on visitors and not on any other responsibility.

❖ Be careful to not be drawn into conversations with those you already know unless you are introducing them to a newcomer.

❖ Turn your radar on as soon as you enter the room. Be alert for those who may be alone, shy, or quiet; are known to be new to the area, to the church, or to the group; and unfamiliar with the building and others present. Many newcomers want to connect with a community of believers but do not know how to do so.

❖ Be gracious, relaxed, and interested in her life. Wear a nametag if possible. Introduce yourself, ask for her name, and remember it during the event. Invite her to sit with you, to join you in something you are doing, or whatever it takes to connect with her more than just saying hello. Key in on common things you share or connect her with someone who shares something in common with her. It is okay to be nosy.

❖ Have something to place in her hand about your church, women's activities, family activities, etc. before she leaves. Invite her back for something specific within a month at least. This could be an all-church event, a women's event, or a children's activity. Find something she might be drawn to attend.

❖ If she reveals specific needs regarding grief, divorce counseling, marriage issues, parenting, singleness, or other common needs, connect her with someone who is similar experiences and has learned to rely on Christ to overcome it.

❖ Make sure you get a way to exchange contact information with her.

AFTER THE EVENT

❖ Follow up with her during the next two weeks. Remember to invite her back for something specific within a month at least. Find something she might be drawn to attend. Meet her at the door when she comes to church for the first time or attends that next event where you will be present.

❖ Pray for her.

❖ That sounds like a lot, but it really is not. Once you have done the preparation, you will use the same stuff at most events you would attend. Invite a friend to join you as a designated engager. Pray together before and after the event. Share this wonderful experience together as you both take the leap into lifestyle disciplemaking!

STAY CHRIST-FOCUSED & TAKE THE NEXT STEPS

Becoming a designated engager is an easy entrance into lifestyle disciplemaking for those of you who love Jesus, love people, and love being friendly to visitors. Does that describe you? Then, I am inviting you to be the "Designated Engager" for your spring tea, women's retreat, or summer Bible study. And please recruit others to join you! How fun can that be for several of you to do this together!

Overcome that tendency for "intentional blindness" at your next women's event. "Turn your radar on" and help a newcomer feel wanted and included! Trust Jesus to help you do that. Then, watch what He does!

When the Holy Spirit gives you opportunity to talk to anyone about Jesus, you need to be ready. We will look at ways that you can prepare to share your faith in the next chapter.

Let Jesus lead you into lifestyle disciplemaking.
Jesus followers become disciplemakers.

TAKE THE LEAP

Thought questions

1. Do you love Jesus and want others to experience the love of Jesus, also? Do you want to be especially friendly to newcomers during an event so they will feel welcomed and wanted? Are you willing to be a designated engager at your next church event where newcomers might be present?

2. Read Matthew 9:36-38. Are you willing to be a harvester in the Lord's harvest?

3. Read Ephesians 6:19 and Colossians 4:5-6. What can you ask Jesus to do for you? Will you trust Him to do this?

4. What could you ask or say to a newcomer that would make her feel wanted and included?

Action steps for individuals

1. Pray about becoming a designated engager for women's events where newcomers would be present.

2. If you feel called to do this, reread the process for being a designated engager included above. Or download the "Designated Engagers Preparation" checklist from melanienewton.com/disciplemaking. Either way, do the preparation necessary to get you ready to be a designated engager at the next event where newcomers might be present. Let your ministry leaders know that you are willing to do this. Ask them for whatever help you need regarding resources to share with a newcomer.

3. If you are not a designated engager but know who they are at your event, you can introduce visitors to them.

4. Be intentionally friendly to any visitor at the events you attend. The more connections she makes, the greater the likelihood that she will come to another event or try attending your church.

5. You can use your designated engager preparation anywhere. Brainstorm through these sample scenarios. What ideas do you have for each case?

    ✓ **Cynical neighbor:** You are pulling weeds when your neighbor comes by. As you visit, you say that you are eager to get the work done today because you will be attending a women's conference at your church tomorrow. She says, "I do not understand what you get out of that church stuff, anyway! No one has all the answers or proof of anything, and all the different religions seem to do is fight and scrap with each other! Don't you think it's a waste of time?" How would you respond?

    ✓ **Worried Wife:** You are talking with the mother of one of your kid's playmates. She seems sad and mentions that she and her husband are splitting up. That really scares her. What could you say to her?

    ✓ **Newcomer to town:** You are in line at a local grocery store. The person in line behind you asks if you know whether or not there is a Home Depot in town. You get the feeling that she is new to your area. She might be experiencing transplant "shock" and is lonely. How would you take advantage of this opportunity?

Action steps for ministry leaders

1. Do you already have a welcome team for your ministries and events? Consider inviting specific women to become "designated engagers" for each event. These would not be greeters at the door or check-in table. They would also not be your small group leaders or table leaders who need to shepherd the whole group.

   - **Invite women** who love Jesus, love other people, and are gifted to be openly friendly. You know who those women are in your group. They would need to be prepared to connect with newcomers as described in the section above for individuals. Encourage the designated engagers to pray together before and after the event.

   - **Train them** to know what they should do as designated engagers. You could follow the same preparation as for individuals, including informing them about what your church offers for grief care, divorce counseling, marriage issues, parenting, singleness, cancer, and other common needs. If you have brochures about those, you can give your engagers a few to keep handy when they attend the events.

   - **Make sure your designated engagers do not have other responsibilities** during an event other than connecting with the newcomers. It is tempting to see someone hanging around and give them a last-minute job to do. Please remember not to do that.

2. **Plan to have designated engagers present** whenever unchurched women are invited to your church or women's event—bazaars, brunches, women's classes, moms' groups, fall festivals, and more.

3. Download the "Designated Engagers Preparation" checklist at melanienewton.com/disciplemaking to use for the women in your small group or church ministry.

Prayer prompts

   ✓ Ask Jesus to give you His love for women who do not know Him and compassion for where they are in life.

✓ Ask Him for boldness and opportunity to interact with newcomers to your event or group.

✓ Ask Him for discernment to know the right words to say in conversation that would make her feel wanted.

✓ Tell Him that you will rely on Him and His Holy Spirit power in you to do this. Then, watch what He does!

What others have done

Amy: "A lot of families move in the summer. If you are looking, you will probably see newly transplanted women in your neighborhood or community who are longing to make new friends. My children and I bake and bag cookies to take to our new neighbors. This gives us an opportunity to connect and share with the neighbors a little about life in that community."

Melissa: "When I am out about town, I make a deliberate practice of looking at the name-tag of the store clerk or other service provider. I try to bring a smile to their faces by greeting them by name (if they have a name tag) and thanking them by name at the end of the transaction. I hope it conveys a message that I consider them valuable to me and to God."

Mary: "We recently held a Spring Tea outreach event. There was definitely some intentional engaging going on at the tea thanks to your spurring us on to love and good deeds!"

Lynn: "I ask for the list of women who are new attendees to our church and write notes to them that say, 'I'm praying for you.' I include my cell number with permission to call or text me any time. I personally deliver the note when I see each woman so I can meet her, begin a relationship with her, and find out where she is spiritually."

Lauren: "Several moms of young children from our church schedule a weekly park date. While there, we intentionally engage the other moms who are not part of our "church group." Since we go to the park regularly, we can let the other moms know when we will be coming back. We intentionally build relationships with them. One has recently started coming to our church. I will say that personally it is easier for me to approach others confidently if I have another friend at the park with me. My friend does not need to go up to a mom with me, but just knowing I am not going at it alone gives me confidence. My husband has even gotten in on it recently as he has seen how easy it is to meet people there at the park."

Erin: "Two friends and I (also young moms) have started meeting regularly to talk about spiritual things, and the next time we meet we'll be talking about how to reach out to our neighbors and friends and will pray and encourage each other as we do it."

Linda: "Our women's ministry team decided we should get a list of all the ladies and divide them up for prayer. I did not know many of the ladies I put on my list. The others did not know them either! That made me realize how badly we needed to do this! So, I wrote notes to each one saying I was praying for them adding my cell number for them to contact me. I hand them out personally so I meet each one and cannot wait to see how God uses these relationships. I have been much better at introducing myself to women when I don't know their names and have made a few friends that are not even on my list."

CHAPTER 4

Prepare to Share Your Faith Story

JESUS FOLLOWERS BECOME DISCIPLEMAKERS

Most of us who have been Christians for any length of time have probably heard Matthew 28:19 where Jesus commissions His disciples to make disciples wherever they are. In my heart, I want to be obedient in sharing about Him to others around me who do not know Him yet or do not know Him well. But I often feel so inadequate. You may feel that way too. This chapter will help you get ready to share your faith in very simple ways.

MAKE GOOD INTENTIONS BECOME INTENTIONAL ACTIONS

So far in this book about lifestyle disciplemaking, we have made the case that Jesus followers become disciplemakers. We covered how to get started by making connections with nonbelievers or just those who are unchurched. To become disciplemakers, we need to go from having good intentions to being intentional at finding and connecting with the nonbelievers in our lives. It starts with identifying who they are, praying for them, and loving them with God's love.

In Chapter 3, we looked at the need for designated engagers who connect with newcomers at any event. That is an easy way to get started with lifestyle disciplemaking. We covered some basic preparation for you to become a designated engager for any church activity and in your community as well.

Soon, you will have made the connections with women who are nonbelievers or unchurched. When the Lord Jesus gives you the opportunity to share your faith, you need to be ready. This chapter will give you ways to prepare to share your faith story so you will be ready.

PARTNERSHIP WITH THE HOLY SPIRIT

A few years ago, I realized that if I was going to get beyond my feeling of inadequacy to share my faith, I would need to work at preparing myself to share about Christ in daily conversation. Once prepared, I would need to ask Him for opportunity to use what I learned to introduce Him to other women and then trust Him to do the rest. By the way, that is the simplicity of lifestyle disciplemaking. It is a huge part of my purpose and your purpose while we are alive on this earth. We are commissioned to follow Jesus as His disciples and live for Him as disciplemakers. But how do we do this?

Remembering this truth takes the pressure off of yourself: **You are in partnership with the Holy Spirit**. He gives you the power to be a witness for Christ (Acts 1:8). You are not on your own! He is at work in you and in the world.

> Evangelism is not about you involving Him in your outreach efforts. It is He involving you in His. Only the Holy Spirit can open the eyes of unbelievers to the truth of the gospel...It is the job of believers to communicate the gospel. It is the job of the Holy Spirit to convert the heart. (David Souther, EvanTell)

TWO POWERFUL RESOURCES

You have two powerful resources to help you fulfill your purpose as you partner with the Spirit. Both are mentioned in what the Spirit inspired John to write in Revelation.

> *They [believers] triumphed over him [Satan] by **the blood of the Lamb** and by **the word of their testimony**. (Revelation 12:11)*

Your two resources are the blood of the Lamb (the gospel message) and the word of your testimony (your faith story). People can reject the facts or logic of the gospel, but it is very hard to argue with someone about their experience of the gospel. Sharing the facts of the gospel and your own faith story are ways to put your faith into words. Sadly, many Christians are not comfortable sharing either! Why is that? I think it is because we do not prepare to do so through practice, encouragement, and experience.

In this chapter and the next one, we will share with you three things you can do on your own to prepare to share your faith so when the Spirit gives you opportunity, you are ready to take it! The first thing is to shape your faith story and practice telling it so it is easy to share. In Chapter 5, we will look at preparing conversation starters and transitions plus knowing the gospel facts.

SHAPING YOUR "FAITH STORY"

Maybe the right words to share your faith story in a conversation come naturally to you. Praise God for that verbal gift! I am willing to declare that for most of us (including me), those words just do not come easily. We do not know where to start. We do not know how much to say. We say too much. Frankly, I have not been in a church yet that stressed the importance of being able to share one's faith story by actually training everyone to do it including frequent opportunities to practice it! Why is that? How many hours do we spend practicing other things but not "the word of our testimony?"

Your story is Jesus' story in your life. Only you know it and can share it. It is your real-life experience of the gospel truth. It is YOUR story—edited by you, filtered by you, and told by you. You can tell it anywhere.

> People love to hear stories. This is evidenced by all the money that is spent watching movies, attending the theatre, buying books and by all the time that is spent watching the television. Telling your faith story is just that: your personal story about your faith. It's an unobtrusive way to speak about the love of God in your life and the love he has for all people...Your life and story is the best tract to be written! (*The Disciplemaking Ministry Guide for Women in Leadership,* "How to Share Your Faith," page 21)

There are several ways to look at telling your faith story. You may recall a dramatic event or specific point in time when you began a personal relationship with Jesus. So, you remember well what it was like to not know Him and the difference He has made in your life.

Or you may have grown up in church and feel like you always knew who God was and trusted in Jesus as your Savior as a child. Those who trusted in Jesus as children often feel they "have nothing to tell" because they do not have a dramatic story. They are unconvinced that their story matters. Yet, in the case of childhood believers, there occurs a later, mature decision to follow Christ as His disciple where more obvious life changes occurred. If you are in this category, focus on that later turning point in telling your story when you made the decision to follow Jesus as His disciple at some point in your teen years or adult life. That is when a childlike faith becomes an adult faith.

By the way, you might consider "nothing to tell" is not sensational enough because you have stayed faithful to Christ through the years. But that kind of faith story is what every parent wants to hear from their own child! You have a story to share! What helped you to stay faithful to Christ?

Here are two ways to shape your faith story so you are ready.

Option 1. Shape your faith story using three words*

When someone gives an easy way to share one's faith story as the opportunity arises, I jump on the idea. The EvanTell ministry provided a three-word exercise for easily telling your faith story in their newsletter. Here is how it works:

❖ Choose any three words to represent (1) your life before trusting in Jesus, (2) how you came to trust in Him, and (3) your life as a believer ever since.

- Choose the **first word** to describe your life, feelings, situation, or thoughts **before** trusting in Christ. Examples: angry, miserable, hopeless, empty, addicted, me-centered, restless, striving, confused, insecure, worried.

  WORD #1 = _____

- Choose the **second word** to describe **how you came to trust** in Christ. Examples: creation, pastor, concert, Bible, friend, evangelist, spouse, teacher, parent.

  WORD #2 = _____

- Choose the **third word** to describe your life, feelings, situation, or thoughts **since** trusting in Christ. Examples: peaceful, loving, trusting, freedom, servant, hopeful, compassionate, confident.

  WORD #3 = _____

❖ Using those three words, create 1-2 sentences for each word—just a brief explanation of how each word relates to your story. A friend of mine gave me the example below using ME-CENTERED, EVANGELIST, and TRUSTING.

Before coming to faith in Jesus Christ, I was ME-CENTERED and thought I was in control of my life. If I wanted something to happen (specifically, get a boyfriend!), I had to make it happen! My sisters came to faith before I did, and through them I saw a lack in my own life. When I heard an EVANGELIST on TV present the gospel, I realized what the lack was. It was a Person, Jesus Christ, and I prayed and asked Him to forgive my sins. Now, I am most blessed in relinquishing control to Him, TRUSTING Him with all my heart, leaning not on my own understanding, acknowledging Him in all my ways, and allowing Him to straighten my paths.

You can interject your 3-word story into a conversation or ask the other person what 3 words might define her life.

Option 2. Shape a 5-minute version of your faith story

Work on your longer story in stages.

❖ **Stage 1: Recall your life before knowing Jesus or choosing to follow Him.** Use these prompts to help you: What were your attitudes, needs, and/or problems? How did those areas or activities begin to disappoint you or leave you unsatisfied? To what source did you look for security, peace of mind, or happiness? Describe how you felt or what your greatest needs were at the time (e.g. loneliness, feelings of insignificance, anger, rejection). Briefly share a personal example from your life that illustrates those needs and attitudes you just identified.

❖ **Stage 2: Recall how you came to know Christ (point of salvation) or chose to follow Him.** Use these prompts to help you: Share when and how you first heard the gospel and/or were exposed to knowing Christ. What brought you to the place of being willing to listen or of wanting to be more than just a believer? Who influenced you? How and when did you decide to follow Jesus? Describe how you felt, what truths you heard, what you thought about them, how you felt after you made the decision.

❖ **Stage 3: Recall the benefits you recognize in your life since knowing Jesus and choosing to follow Him.** Use these prompts to help you. What conditions before you really knew Christ have been satisfied by a relationship with Him? What does it look like in your life to have a relationship with Christ? How long did it take before you noticed changes? What does it look like in your life to have this closer relationship with Christ? What are your blessings since having Jesus in your life? Where do you struggle still? How do you depend on Jesus through those struggles? Briefly share a personal example from your life that illustrates the wonderful difference that Jesus Christ has made in your life.

Script something you can share in about 5 minutes.

❖ Whether you like to be spontaneous or need everything written down, it helps to script what you will say. It forces you to think through what you will say to maintain your main idea. It helps you to manage your allowed time. Spend only about **30% of the time on your "before,"** just enough to have them identify with your need at that time. Spend **another 30% on the decision time,** and spend **the rest of the time on what knowing Christ has done for you**. Always end inviting them to join your adventure.

❖ Write it as you would speak it with shorter sentences using everyday words that are clear and simple. Include specific illustrations that give them snapshots of your life, not only general descriptions of your life events. Screen your language for churchy words that an unchurched person might not understand. Practice saying your story several times. You can use a mirror to practice making eye contact with the listener to draw her into your story. Get together with friends and have a "Tell Your Story" party.

STAY CHRIST-FOCUSED & TAKE THE NEXT STEPS

Jesus is drawing men and women to Himself. He commissions you to be part of the process of introducing them to Him. When the Holy Spirit gives you opportunity to talk to anyone about Jesus, you need to be ready. We will look at ways that you can prepare conversation starters and transitions plus sharing the gospel facts in the next chapter. Trust Jesus to help you do this. Then, watch what He does!

Let Jesus lead you into lifestyle disciplemaking. Jesus followers become disciplemakers.

TAKE THE LEAP

Thought questions

1. Read Acts 21:39-22:21. When Paul got an opportunity to share his story, he took it. He had already thought through what he would share so he was ready. If given the opportunity to share

your story, do you want to be ready? Will you commit to being ready?

2. Before you trusted in Christ, did you hear others sharing their faith stories that drew you to Jesus? To what part of their story were you mostly drawn?

3. What has Jesus done in your life? What is it like to have a relationship with Him? How do you know He is real and what you have learned is true?

4. If you grew up in the church and stayed faithful to Jesus for the most part until now, you have the story every parent of young children wants to hear! What influenced you to stay faithful?

5. If given the opportunity by the Holy Spirit to briefly share with an unbeliever about your relationship with Jesus, what would you say in less than 5 minutes? Consider two ways that knowing Jesus has made a difference in your life, given you hope, restored something lost, etc.

Action steps for individuals

1. Start shaping your faith story using either tool given in this chapter. Or you can download the "Prepare to Share" booklet from melanienewton.com/disciplemaking, which includes both the 3-word and 5-minute faith story worksheets.

   - Work on your 3-word story and / or your 5-minute faith story.
   - Practice sharing your faith story often.

2. Invite some Christian friends to shape their 3-word or 5-minute faith story. Have a "Tell Your Story" party with them. Make it fun. Rejoice with one another and give glory to God as you see His creativity in drawing each one of you to Him.

3. **If you are a small group leader:** As you review your lesson and make a plan for leading the discussion, consider where you could easily and quickly share part of your story.

Action steps for ministry leaders

1. Give the women in your ministry the simple tools to work on their faith stories. Then, have a faith-story sharing party. Break up into groups of 4-5 so each one can share her story with the rest of the group members in less than half an hour. Choose a couple of women to share their stories with the whole group. Be sure to

include one person who stayed true to Christ from childhood as well as the one who did not know Him until they were an adult.

2. Incorporate faith story sharing as part of your next retreat, all-day conference, or Bible study lecture time.

3. Provide help for anyone needing help. Have a group of ladies willing to read through what others have written and give feedback.

4. **If you are a small group leader:** Give opportunity for your group members to share their 3-word or 5-minute faith stories as a group activity. Give them the "Prepare to Share Your Faith" booklet ahead of time so they can prepare. Do the sharing during group time where it fits in with the lesson, or plan a group get together over dinner or dessert where there is plenty of time for each one to share her story.

Prayer prompts

✓ Ask the Lord to help you write your faith story, what to include, and how to invite someone to open her heart to hear it.

✓ Ask Him to give you opportunity to share it soon.

What others have done

Tara: "While my son is at soccer practice and during games, I intentionally sit next to one of the moms, Michelle, who is not liked by the other moms mostly because of her immoral lifestyle (living with her boyfriend). But, over the months as we have laughed together and enjoyed each other's company, we have become friends. From the beginning, my husband and I have prayed for Michelle and her boyfriend as a couple, asking the Lord to reveal Himself to them. I invited Michelle to walk with me so we have added that time together as well. By spending time together, I have listened to her life story and tried to understand why she thinks the way she does. Michelle attended our women's ministry outreach event, a spring tea, and enjoyed it. She and her boyfriend even came to Easter service together and lunch with us afterwards. Michelle knows I care about her and is now open to listening about Christ. It has taken time (months) and a lot of intentional effort. I contacted Michelle 5 different ways to connect with her: side-by-side sitting, Facebook, texting, calling to invite her for walks, and dropping by her house. Believe in breakthroughs for nonbelievers!"

Marilyn: "After learning about lifestyle disciplemaking, I went back to my church and invited the other women to start working on their 5-minute faith stories to share with each other in a Sunday morning class. So I worked on my own story, then the Lord gave me an opportunity to share it a week later with a neighbor who trusted in Christ after hearing it."

Brandi: "The women in our church decided to practice telling our faith stories by way of email rather than at a planned gathering. This worked surprisingly well because the women who participated shared things that no one would otherwise ever know. The story sharing became a bonding experience for everyone who participated."

Erica: "We had a meaningful, fun time at your workshop. Your wisdom, experience, and enthusiasm is contagious. Our table group and possibly a few others are meeting next weekend to practice our testimonies and strategies."

CHAPTER 5

Prepare to Share the Gospel Facts

JESUS FOLLOWERS BECOME DISCIPLEMAKERS

W ho told you about Jesus so that you could know Him? Was it a parent? A Sunday School teacher? A friend? Whoever it was, they shared the Good News with you. You received it and had your life changed because of knowing Him. It is your turn to be that bearer of that good news to someone else who needs to know Jesus or needs to know Him better. In Chapter 4, we encouraged you to shape your faith story and practice telling it. In this chapter, we will look at preparing conversation starters and transitions where you can interject parts of your faith story and share the gospel facts when the Spirit gives you the opportunity.

It is important for you and me to not only be confident in our own understanding of the gospel but also to be able to clearly communicate the gospel truth to everyone in our sphere of influence. You may get only one week influencing a teen at youth camp, but your mentoring might be the catalyst for that person to stay strong in his or her walk with Christ for years to come. Our role in disciplemaking is not to try to fix their problems but to point them to Jesus who gives new life and the strength to face anything this world throws at us. It is all about a relationship with Him.

TWO POWERFUL RESOURCES

You have two powerful resources to help you fulfill your purpose as you partner with the Holy Spirit in telling others about Christ. Both are mentioned in what the Spirit inspired John to write in Revelation.

> *They [believers] triumphed over him [Satan] by **the blood of the Lamb** and **by the word of their testimony**. (Revelation 12:11)*

Your two resources are the blood of the Lamb (the gospel message) and the word of your testimony (your faith story). People can reject the facts or logic of the gospel, but it is very hard to argue with someone about their experience of the gospel. Sharing the facts of the gospel and your own faith story are ways to put your faith into words. Sadly, many Christians are not comfortable sharing either! Why is that? As I said in the last chapter, we do not prepare to do so through practice, encouragement, and experience.

USE CONVERSATION STARTERS

Paul wrote to the Colossians,

> *Be wise in the way you act toward outsiders; make the most of every opportunity. Let **your conversation be always full of grace, seasoned with salt,** so that you may know how to answer everyone. (Colossians 4:5-6)*

Basically, he said to create some salty conversation. That means you should be ready with some conversation starters when you encounter someone outside of your Christian circle.

Maybe the right words to share your faith in a conversation come naturally to you. Praise God for that verbal gift! Yet, for most of us (including me), those words just do not come easily. I have to prepare ahead of time.

What are some good conversation starters to stimulate meaningful talk that might reveal a woman's heart and give you a chance to invite it somewhere? Usually, these are general questions that you can ask anyone—your hairdresser, coworker, neighbor, or restaurant server. Think about what someone used the first time they peeked your interest about spiritual things.

These are a few examples that others have shared with me:

- What were you taught about God while growing up?
- What do you do when you feel defeated?
- What are some of your joys in this season of life?
- What challenges and struggles are you facing?
- If you could tell a favorite part of your life story, what would it be?
- Will you please tell me about your tattoo?

You can probably think of several more. It just takes 1 or 2 to connect with someone and get them sharing with you.

PREPARE CONVERSATION TRANSITIONS

Once a conversation gets started, you will need to have some prepared transitions from common topics of casual conversation that could lead into meaningful conversation about your faith.

What are some **transitions that could lead into sharing your story**? Consider how you might identify with her and what God has done in your life to make the difference.

Paul wrote this in 1 Corinthians.

*Yes, I try to **find common ground** with everyone, doing everything I can to save some. (1 Corinthians 9:22 NLT)*

That was his practice. It can be ours as well.

Examples of conversation transitions

Here are some examples of conversation transitions from common topics. Consider how you would finish each sentence related to a common topic.

- *Corruption, evil and sin:* "Though I am not guilty of that particular sin, I am just as guilty of…"

- *Community:* "I believe we are created by God to live in a real community, first of all with Him. And I have experienced this…"

- *Family:* "I am so glad that God cares even more about my family than I do. What would I do without Him helping me to…"

- *Something good happened:* "God has been so kind to you in that. I saw His kindness to me when…"

- *Pain & suffering:* "Yes. I understand how that really hurts…"

- *High expectations:* "I am so glad God does not expect perfection from me. What a relief it is to know how He loves me just as I am…"

- *Anger at someone:* "I love the way God is changing me from the inside out. Not too long ago, I would have been so upset by that, but now when I am angry or hurt…"

- *Church ("I don't go to church."):* "Going to church is not what it is really about for me. I just find that the closer I get to Jesus the more content my heart is and…"

You can probably think of several more. The point is that you can think through some conversation starters and transitions that lead into sharing some part of your story. Ask the Spirit to give you boldness and opportunity to use them.

Responding to those who have been hurt by Christians

As we reach out to the unchurched around us, we will run across people who have had a bad experience with Christians or the church (or see something in the news that gives Christianity a "black eye"). How do we respond to that?

Here are four things to keep in mind as you relate to that person (adapted from *The Evangelism Study Bible*):

- Do not be defensive. Yes, there are hypocritical Christians who are serving themselves more than serving God.

- Remind them there are fakes in every area of society. Few would stop cheering for a favorite football team because of a corrupt player.

- Remind them that the Good News is about Jesus, not Christians. It is about a relationship with Someone who loves them dearly.

- Introduce them personally to Christians who do live for Christ.

Counter negative comments by being prepared with positive comments of your own as in the *Conversation Transitions* above.

PREPARE TO SHARE THE GOSPEL FACTS

The gospel message is good news. It is very simple. God made it that way. You do not need to know every aspect of theology to share the gospel. The gospel is an announcement to the world of an accomplished fact. What God set out to do for humans, He accomplished. Salvation is available on the basis of a single condition. That one condition is faith in Jesus Christ.

What faith is

The word "faith" means a "belief, trust, and commitment of mind and heart to something or someone."

- Faith is **intelligent**. That means first you need to know about the something or someone. It is based on information about the object of your faith.

- Faith is also **decisive**. It involves the element of assent or agreement that the information about that someone or something is true.

- Faith requires an **act of the will**. Any conscious choice that involves trust or dependence on someone or something requires a deliberate action to both trust the information and act on it. It is the difference between walking alongside a pool of water (seeing it is there) and jumping into the water (experiencing the water personally).

Notice that faith begins with knowing the truth about someone. **The gospel facts reveal the truth**. The listener has to agree with that information, to agree it is true. Then, the response is an act of the will—a commitment to trust in the information.

It is the job of believers to communicate the gospel. It is the job of the Holy Spirit to convert the heart. (David Souther, EvanTell)

You and I are to simply communicate the truth. In order to do that effectively, we can learn and practice a simple way to share the gospel message so you will be ready when given an opportunity.

If you remember, how did someone share the gospel message with you? What have you used to share the gospel message with others?

As it is written: "How beautiful are the feet of those who **bring good news!**" (Romans 10:15)

Bring that good news to those on your "Pray and Love" list and other connections you have made where there is opportunity to share the gospel.

We speak as those approved by God to be **entrusted with the gospel.** (1 Thessalonians 2:4)

You have been entrusted with the gospel. It is a treasure you can share with others.

Choose a simple presentation to learn.

Choose a simple presentation of the gospel to memorize and have ready to use when given the opportunity by the Spirit of God in your daily life. Speak it aloud to yourself several times so you know it well without really having to think about it. Ask the Spirit to give you boldness and opportunity to share this with someone soon.

HERE IS ONE EXAMPLE USING JOHN 3:16

Has anyone introduced you to Jesus so you could know Him? May I? *Read John 3:16.* This tells of...

❖ **God's Love:** *"For God so loves you __(name)__ ..."* God loves you and created you to enjoy a relationship with Him. But sin prevents you from experiencing this relationship. You cannot be good enough on your own to overcome this sin barrier and its penalty of death. God's love led to...

❖ **God's Gift:** *"God gave His one and only Son"* Jesus to live as one of us then to take our penalty for sin on Himself when He died on the cross. Our sins could now be forgiven. He was then raised from the dead to be alive again and to give us His life. Because the price for our sin has been paid, the way to God is clear and simple through...

❖ **God's Offer:** *"Whoever believes in Him shall not perish but have eternal life ..."* That means to trust in God's loving plan, accept what Jesus did on the cross for you, admit your sin, and desire a relationship with Him. To perish means to die separated from God and His love for you. Eternal life means you can enjoy a forever-family relationship with God now and after your life on earth ends.

❖ When offered a gift you want, you take it and say thank you. It is forever yours. Is anything keeping you from trusting in Jesus right now? Would you like to pray now and tell God you are accepting His love gift of salvation in Jesus?

After sharing the facts, you can invite her to pray this prayer along with you:

Thank you, God, for loving me and for sending Your Son Jesus to die for my sins. I trust in Jesus Christ to be my personal Savior. I accept your gift of forgiveness for my sins. I turn my life over to You. Thank you for your goodness to me and your gift of eternal life. Amen.

If she does that, celebrate with her. And give her this assurance:

As soon as you trust in Christ to be your Savior, you begin a loving relationship with Him. You receive complete love and acceptance by God as your Father. You receive treasure that is yours to know and experience for the rest of your earthly life. When you trust in Christ, He is in your life forever. You will never be without him. Ever.

STAY CHRIST-FOCUSED & TAKE THE NEXT STEPS

We have covered several ways to CONNECT with nonbelievers and share the gospel with them. Trust Jesus to help you do this. Then, watch what He does!

What do you do when that person trusts in Christ? ESTABLISH is the next phase in the process of disciplemaking. New believers need to be established in their faith. That is the subject of the next chapter.

Let Jesus lead you into lifestyle disciplemaking. Jesus followers become disciplemakers.

TAKE THE LEAP

Thought questions

1. If you remember, how did someone share the gospel message with you? How did they start the conversation? What peaked your interest?

2. How would you finish the conversation transitions from common topics we included in this chapter?

3. What have you used to share the gospel message with others?

4. How do you respond to those who have been hurt by Christians in the past?

Action steps for individuals

1. Prepare conversation starters and transitions to use in casual conversation. Consider the parts of your story that might identify with another woman whom you might encounter. Think of good questions to ask or statements to make that would reveal a woman's heart. Practice saying them while driving in the car or taking a shower or whenever you have time. Now, ask God for the opportunity to use your salt seasoning soon in a conversation with an unchurched person. You can download the "Prepare to Share" booklet from my website (melanienewton.com/disciplemaking), which includes the *Conversation Transitions* worksheet.

2. What would make you less uncomfortable about sharing the gospel with someone? The answer is "practice." Learn a simple presentation of the gospel message. Find a way that works for you. Write it on a card and practice it over and over until you know it backwards and forwards. Challenge yourself to learn it well. You can download the "Prepare to Share" booklet from my website, which includes several ways to share the gospel.

3. If you learn best from videos, EvanTell.org offers some online video training to share the gospel message.

4. Practice sharing the gospel facts with friends. The more you speak it, the easier it will be to remember what to say when the time comes.

Action steps for ministry leaders

1. Provide a simple way to share the gospel facts to everyone in your ministry. Ask them to learn it then host a gospel sharing practice time. Let them break up into groups of 4-5 and practice sharing the gospel with each other. Afterward, offer some role-play scenarios for the whole group to watch.

2. Many people learn best from videos. EvanTell.org offers some online video training to share the gospel message. You can show it to the whole group then practice it in smaller groups afterwards.

3. Brainstorm through these sample scenarios as a group or in smaller groups. What ideas do you have for each case?

   ▪ **Atheist Alice:** Alice is your coworker. She grew up without any spiritual foundation and believes there is no God. She is now a divorced mother of two girls. She believes that she can get strength from within herself whenever she needs it, digging down deep. She also believes that she has enough help from her friends so she does not need anything spiritual. Her Facebook posts show that she manages life's challenges through frequent margaritas. Discuss ways you can connect with Alice and non-threatening questions you could ask to lead her to thinking about spiritual needs in her life.

   ▪ **Kind Kathy:** Kathy is your neighbor. She is very friendly. She shows on her Facebook page that she supports Christian events and ideas. Yet, she is living with a man who is not her husband. They stay very active on weekends and do not attend church. They are good neighbors and respond well when you invite them to get together with you, although their schedule is pretty packed so it does not happen easily. Discuss how you could more intentionally connect with Kathy and take advantage of her familiarity with Christianity.

- **Skeptical Sheri:** You (believing friend) play tennis in a city tennis league so you can keep in shape and interact with nonbelievers. Sheri is your weekly tennis partner. Sheri is openly skeptic about anything dealing with Christianity. She was raised in a church setting but drifted seriously away during college. She is an intellectual who thinks Jesus was just a good teacher. She does pursue various activities such as Zen meditation to meet her spiritual needs. Discuss ways you can connect with Sheri in meaningful conversation.

Prayer prompts

✓ Commit your fears to Jesus and trust Him to give you the opportunity to share His good news with at least one person. If you do not feel confident, that is okay because you will depend on Him more. Feel free to say, *"I can't do this on my own, Lord Jesus, but You can do this through me. I will trust you."*

✓ Ask Him to help you live dependently on Him and to recognize the opportunities He gives you to share what you have practiced.

✓ Ask Him to do His part which is to draw people to Himself.

✓ Ask Him to help you be ready to introduce Him to those He draws. That is your part.

What others have done

Donna: "My husband and I stayed at a bed and breakfast and found out that the owner was going in for breast cancer treatments early the next week. When she found out that I was a breast cancer survivor, there was an immediate bonding. I was able to encourage her before we left. She sent us a thank you card for staying there and thanked me for my encouragement. She had expressed a deep fear of her situation, so I continued to encourage her through email correspondence. I am praying that she will stay in touch, and I will be able to continue to have input into her life. None of this would have happened if I had not attended your Lifestyle Disciplemaking training. I was open and ready to engage those with whom God brought me into contact."

Alice: "I was hoping to reach out to my neighbors, and I have had the chance to do that with a few of them one-on-one. This week I am inviting the ladies on my street for coffee. I do not know why, but I have been afraid to go ahead and invite them (I am still fearful now). But I am going to be courageous and do it anyway because I know the Holy Spirit is leading me to invite them. Please pray that this time would be a blessing to all who attend and that conversations might lead to good friendships and sharing the love of Christ."

Establish New and Young Christians

CHAPTER 6

Give Believers Strong Roots

JESUS FOLLOWERS BECOME DISCIPLEMAKERS

When you trusted in Christ, were you discipled as a new believer to help you understand the basics of Christianity? If not, have you struggled in your faith? New and young believers need to be established in their faith. In reality, every Christian needs to have a strong foundation that provides strong roots. Strong roots prevent instability and insecurity. Jesus modeled how to establish believers in the truth. We can follow His example as we intentionally disciple new and never-been-discipled Christians among our friends and church family. New and young believers need to know some basic truths to grow spiritually strong.

JESUS MODELED HOW TO ESTABLISH BELIEVERS IN THE TRUTH

During the last two years of His earthly ministry, Jesus intentionally taught His 12 disciples and many others to know Him, to follow Him, and to obey Him. He established them in truth He wanted them to know.

> To establish means "to build a solid foundation; to provide strong roots."

Establish is a good word to describe growing in your faith. That is what Jesus did for everyone who had committed to follow Him as a disciple. He established them in truth and what it means to apply that truth in obedience to God.

In Chapter 1, we defined a **disciple** as an active follower or learner. If you follow Jesus as His disciple, you are making the choice to learn from Jesus through what is taught in the Bible and apply those teachings to your life.

We tend to focus on the healing miracles in the gospels. But Jesus spent more time teaching people than just healing. Often, the teaching came first.

> *When Jesus landed and saw a large crowd, he had compassion*
> *on them, because they were like sheep without a shepherd. So*
> *he **began teaching them** many things. (Mark 6:34)*

Jesus taught in many villages, both in the synagogues and out in the open. Matthew records for us examples of the sermons that Jesus gave—solid teaching of truth. The gospels also record parables He told as illustrations of biblical truth. His audience included men, women, and children. Quite a few stayed close to listen to every word, including His 12 disciples. And women were getting established in the truth in the same way that the men were.

First, we can see that Jesus taught them truth based on Old Testament scriptures. He highlighted what they needed to know as truth and countered any error they had been taught by some of the Jewish leaders. Then, He challenged them to apply what He taught them in obedience to God. After His death and resurrection, a group of 120 men and women were prepared and waiting for the Holy Spirit to come (Acts 1:12-15; 2:1-4). No longer able to visibly see the Lord, they learned to depend on the Spirit living inside of them to continue teaching them the truths they needed to know about their new life in Christ.

On the day of Pentecost, the Lord added 3000 new believers to their number. All those new believers needed to be established in their faith. The Apostles did that through consistent teaching.

> *They devoted themselves **to the apostles' teaching** and to*
> *fellowship, to the breaking of bread and to prayer. (Acts 2:42)*

Generation after generation, God has used mature Christians to establish new believers in the truths of the faith, down to the teachers who taught you truth to establish you and give you roots as a Christian. New and young believers need to be established in their faith. In reality, every Christian needs to have a strong foundation that provides strong roots. Strong roots prevent instability and insecurity.

> *So Christ Himself gave the apostles, the prophets, the*
> *evangelists, the **pastors and teachers,** to equip His people for*
> *works of service, so that the body of Christ may be built up until*
> *we all reach unity in the faith and in the knowledge of the Son*
> *of God and **become mature**, attaining to the whole measure of*
> *the fullness of Christ. Then we will **no longer be infants**, tossed*
> *back and forth by the waves, and blown here and there by every*

wind of teaching and by the cunning and craftiness of people in their deceitful scheming. (Ephesians 4:11-14)

Establishing believers helps them to become mature in Christ and provides protection from deception. The ESTABLISH phase of lifestyle disciplemaking is just as important as the CONNECT phase.

ESTABLISH NEW AND YOUNG BELIEVERS

As disciplemakers, we are to not only share our faith and lead others to trust in Christ, but we are also to establish them so they will get rooted in their Christian faith. I read this several years ago:

> Once people trust Christ, do not leave them alone! New believers who begin the Christian life are at a critical point. Leaving the old life behind isn't easy. Though the Holy Spirit provides the power to live victoriously, old patterns, old habits, and old temptations are still there. They need mature believers to walk alongside them while they take their first steps on the road to maturity. As a bare minimum, new believers need discipleship a minimum of once a week for eight weeks. The first eight weeks are sometimes when new converts face their greatest adjustments, strongest temptations, and biggest doubts. To have a brother or sister in Christ meeting with them makes a marked difference...When you follow-up with new believers, they are less concerned with how much you know and more concerned with how much you care. (Evantell.org)

Wow! Establishing new believers right away is critical. Paul wrote about the importance of this in his letter to the Colossians.

> *So then, just as you received Christ Jesus as Lord, continue to live your lives in him, **rooted and built** up in him, **strengthened in the faith** as you were taught, and overflowing with thankfulness. (Colossians 2:6-7)*

New Christians need to be rooted and connected

The goal of establishing a new or young believer is to help her get **rooted in the basics of the faith** and **connected with the community of believers** to continue learning. Your willingness to help new believers around you get rooted in their faith flows out of your love for God and love for His people.

69

When Jesus places a new Christian in your life, what are your options? You can invite her to church, class, or small group and assume she will "catch on" to what she needs to know. But is that the best way? Yes, you want her to join a community of believers, but she needs you right there beside her, personally discipling her in the basics of what it means to be a Christian. That is the best way.

New Christians need spiritual milk

Think of your new Christian friend like she is a hungry newborn baby. They need spiritual milk—regular feeding on the milk of God's Word in order to grow.

> Like **newborn babies,** *crave pure* **spiritual milk,** *so that by it you may* **grow up** *in your salvation, (1 Peter 2:2)*

Picture bringing a newborn baby home and sitting her at the table saying, "Watch the rest of us eat. You will learn how to feed yourself and not be hungry anymore." Do we do that? No! We feed them regularly with nourishing milk and bathe them with parental love for months so they will be healthy physically and relationally. Parents do the feeding with milk first then by introducing solid food. After that, parents start giving them finger foods they can handle. By the middle of their second year, the babies are usually feeding themselves from the table using a mouthful of teeth to do so. Yet, because new Christians are in grown bodies, we expect them to feed themselves from God's Word just by being "at the table" (attending church or being in a small group).

Through the years, I have been in some good Bible teaching churches. A couple of them have had occasional classes for new believers to get the basics of the faith. But none of them have offered tools and the push for me to personally disciple a new believer (or a Christian who has never been discipled) to know God, what Christ did for them on the cross, and their identity in Christ. It seems like that would be an essential part of church ministry. Instead, the assumption is that if someone comes to church or Bible study, they will get what they need to know by just participating. But do they? This lack of nurture of new Christians can lead to discouragement and insecurity and a feeling of "I am not smart enough to understand anything." They miss the joy of spiritual growth.

New Christians need basic training

Just as a newborn baby needs to know the love and trustworthiness of her parents, the new Christian needs to know and experience the love and trustworthiness of her God. She needs to know some basics of the Christian faith, laying a good foundation of truth for her to grasp and apply to her life.

Consider how we prepare children to know certain basics before entering kindergarten—letters and numbers, some personal hygiene (using the toilet, washing their hands, using a tissue). Compare that effort with how we typically assimilate new Christians into the local church.

What assumptions do we make when we invite a new Christian to church or a small group? We assume they already have a Bible and know how to look up a verse. Bad assumption. We can no longer assume that women have been taught any truth about Jesus, the Bible, the Church, or the Christian life. The Lord wants mature Christians like you and I to be willing to establish new and young believers so they can grow strong roots.

GIVE THEM SOME BASIC BIBLE READING SKILLS

The Bible is God's Word for every new Christian so she can get to know God well. Because so many women today were not raised in a church setting, assume the one you are discipling does not know much about it. Anyone who is new to Christ or new to the Bible needs to know some basic skills so she can read and study a Bible.

Make sure the one you are discipling has a Bible (print or app) in a good translation that she can understand. Lead her to find an easy-to-read Bible translation such as NIV, ESV, CSB, NLT, or NET. Avoid the paraphrase versions at first (e.g., The Message, The Passion Translation). "The Bible App (from Life.Church)" is a good one to use. Help her to get the right app, not any copycat versions that have popup ads.

Several years ago, I was in a Sunday School class studying through Romans. When we got to Romans 13:13, someone read it in her King James Version, "Let us walk honestly, as in the day; not in rioting and drunkenness, not in chambering and wantonness." Several of us said, "Huh? What is chambering?" One lady said the word chambering today means putting ammunition in a weapon. In the 1600s when the KJV was completed, chambering referred to prostitution and sexual immorality. Many people have old Bibles that were given to them as children, usually in the King James Version. Mature Christians can handle the difficult language, but newborn Christians have trouble. That is one reason why you need to make sure she has a Bible translation she can understand.

Explain to her that the Bible is one book containing a collection of 66 books combined together for our benefit. It is divided into two main parts: Old Testament and New Testament. The Old Testament tells the story of the beginning of the world and God's promises to mankind given through the nation of Israel. It tells how the people of Israel obeyed and disobeyed God over many years. All the stories and messages in the Old Testament lead up to Jesus Christ's coming to the earth. The New Testament tells the story of Jesus Christ, the early Christians, and God's promises to all those who believe in Jesus. You can think of the Old Testament as "before Christ came" and the New Testament as "after Christ came."

Tell her that each book of the Bible is divided into chapters and verses within those chapters to make it easier to study. Bible references include the book name, chapter number, and verse number(s). For example, Ephesians 2:8 refers to the New Testament book of Ephesians, the 2nd chapter, and verse 8 within that 2nd chapter.

Show her how to use the table of contents of her Bible or Bible app to find specific books of the Bible to read. Some Bible apps let you find books in alphabetical order so you do not need to know if it is in the Old or New Testament.

Walk through a chapter from the gospel of Mark with her. Show her how to read the passage and let the Holy Spirit show her something from it. I usually ask the question, "What grabbed your attention?" That is the milk God wants to feed her that day.

Our *Graceful Beginnings* books for anyone new to the Bible have a "Bible Basics" section covering these helpful skills for new believers.

One friend of mine who became a believer as an adult said that she got herself a children's Bible and read through it. That made it easy for her to get the gist of the Bible stories that everyone else seemed to know. I thought that was a great idea!

INTRODUCE WHAT ALL BELIEVERS NEED TO KNOW

When a child begins piano lessons, the teacher explains what the lines and notes on the page of music represent, what sharps and flats are, and which notes are meant for the right and left hands. That is basic music theory. Likewise, for new believers in Christ, we need to make sure they get the basics in an organized fashion from someone who personally cares about them.

Although excellent resources exist that you can use to help them get rooted in their faith, they need a relationship with another Christian more than just having the right materials. Walking alongside new believers in their first steps of spiritual growth takes time and hard work. But maybe you can be the nurturer to help them develop strong roots of faith that will hold through the years. And in the process, you find out how much you really know and understand about your own faith.

Here are eight essentials of a good foundation for every believer (new or long-term) to be "rooted and built up in Him, strengthened in the faith."

1) Who Christ is, what He has done for us on the cross, and what His resurrection means for us

The most important thing a believer should know and understand is Christ. Christianity is Christ! It is not a lifestyle or rules of conduct. It is not a society whose members were initiated by the sprinkling or covering of water. It is about Jesus Christ and our relationship with Him. What all believers need first and foremost is to get to know Him well and be secure in their relationship with Him.

I spent some time a few years back evaluating resources available online for establishing new believers in the basics of their new faith). What I discovered is that many jump right away from "hooray, you are a Christian now" to "do this or God is going to be unhappy with you when you do anything wrong." I bristled at that!

Why would you jump right away into confession of sin and obedience, skipping Jesus? I do not get it! They need to know who Jesus is first and foremost. If you are discipling a new believer, get them reading the gospel of Mark right away. It is the shortest gospel and the easiest to understand.

A new believer also needs to know what Christ did for her on the cross in His death and what His resurrection gives to her. Forgiveness, reconciliation, and justification are benefits we receive from the cross and are huge relationship changers when it comes to our relationship with God. The new life she gets because of Jesus' resurrection begins the moment she trusts in Christ and continues forever. She needs that assurance.

2) Who the Holy Spirit is and how He works in our lives

The Holy Spirit is God's empowering presence in her life. Make sure she understands that He is a person living inside of her who is actively involved in her life. He is the one helping her to understand the Bible passages she is reading. He is the one representing Jesus to her and leading her to trust Him. The Spirit is the one who produces fruit in her life and helps her to sense God's presence with her and His love for her. He is there whether she "feels" it or not.

3) Living by the Spirit's power rather than living by the flesh

Faith is how she received Christ and His Holy Spirit giving her new life. Faith is how she turns her life over to Jesus and trusts Him on a daily basis. Christianity is not a set of rules to follow on her own. She needs to know and understand God's grace toward her and what it means to live in the freedom of that grace. The Christian life is a life of becoming more dependent on God and less independent of Him. It is a different way of approaching life than what the world teaches.

4) What prayer is and knowing God the Father's love

Even if she did not have a good earthly father, she can by faith believe that she has a good Heavenly Father who loves her dearly and delights in her relying upon Him through prayer. Jesus taught His followers to think of God as their Heavenly Father. The Bible repeatedly calls Christians "dearly loved children" of God (Ephesians 5:1; Colossians 3:12). Dearly loved!

She needs to know that prayer is simply communicating with her Heavenly Father and hearing back from Him through what He says in the Bible. It is conversation with Someone who loves her dearly. What a privilege for the believer to go directly into God's presence and talk with Him about whatever is on her heart. He desires to hear from her, and He promises to listen.

5) Your identity in Christ

The moment she believed, the old self that was born in Adam died. A new self with the same body but a new interior started life as a new person with a new nature "in Christ." That new identity contains many unconditional benefits that she got all at once the moment she trusted in Christ. These benefits make possible an unending relationship with God as her Father. One of the fundamental questions of the human race is that of identity, "Who am I?" The one secure, eternal answer is that through faith in Jesus Christ she can say, "I am in Christ, a child of God, one of God's saints, completely loved and accepted by God." That is an identity that no circumstance can change.

6) Obedience to God flowing from love and gratitude rather than obligation

The entire Christian life is to be lived by faith not by performance (works). Other religions force their followers to adhere to a list of rules to stay acceptable to their deities. Christians should want to obey God out of love and gratitude for how much God loves us and for Jesus paying the ultimate price for our sins. Yet, we cannot live an obedient Christian life in our own strength. We must live by faith in Christ every day. By faith, we trust the Holy Spirit to enable us to obey what God wants for our lives. By faith, we learn to obey Christ and experience a life of freedom and joy.

7) Being part of the Body of Christ and enjoying its community

What a privilege it is to enjoy fellowship with God through fellowship with other believers in God's awesome family on earth— the Church (usually written with a capital "C" to distinguish from local individual churches). While she is part of the universal Church, God wants her to be part of a local church family. It is like having relatives all over the world but living with your immediate family. A local church is a group of believers committed to worshiping Christ, teaching and learning from His Word, supporting each other as they follow Jesus together, and proclaiming the good news to others. She can enjoy relationships and spiritual growth within a local church community.

8) Telling others about Jesus

As a follower of Jesus Christ, she now has the awesome privilege of sharing the good news of eternal life with others. There is tremendous joy in reaching out to those who do not know Jesus and introducing them to Him so they can know Him just as she now knows Him. This includes letting others see how Christ is living His life through you. And it also includes telling the good news of the gospel. If she has opportunity to tell someone one thing, she can tell them what she knows about Jesus. That is enough to plant the seed.

Resources for new Christians

Our *A Fresh Start Bible Study* is designed for new Christians and covers all of the basic information given above. We have several other sources to recommend for new Christians on my website (melanienewton.com/disciplemaking). Even a young believer when provided good resources can walk a new believer through what we just called the basics.

STAY CHRIST-FOCUSED & TAKE THE NEXT STEPS

Lifestyle disciplemaking starts with connecting with nonbelievers so you can introduce them to Jesus. It continues with helping the women in your life who are new or never-been-discipled Christians to become established in their faith. As we get to know our neighbors, coworkers, children's friends, or classmates, we will run across women whose lives look like they are nonbelievers. After getting to know them better, we find out they may have trusted Christ as children but never were discipled to know the truths about their new identity and way of living in Christ. They know they are saved and going to heaven when they die but not much else. No wonder they get tossed back and forth by every new idea that comes along. They are missing out on a life of freedom and joy!

Carefully feed the new Christian what she needs to grow to become established in her faith. Are you willing to do that for someone? So where do you find someone to disciple? And how do you get started? In the next chapter, we will explore your choice to disciple others. Trust Jesus to help you do this. Then, watch what He does!

Let Jesus lead you into lifestyle disciplemaking. Jesus followers become disciplemakers.

TAKE THE LEAP

Thought questions

1. What assumptions do you make when you invite a new Christian or unchurched person to attend church or small group with you?

2. If you trusted in Christ as an adult, did you go to a class for new Christians or were personally discipled? If your answer is yes to either question, what did they use to establish you in the faith?

3. As you read the 8 components of a solid foundation, have you been rooted with this basic information? Was anything new to you? Do you recognize some gaps in your understanding? What would you like to know?

4. How are the basics of the faith being taught in your church or your home?

5. Does your church offer a new believers' class? If not, would you prayerfully consider leading one to establish them in their faith?

Action steps for individuals

1. If you are a new believer, we recommend that you work through *A Fresh Start Bible Study* which covers the 8 essential truths described in this chapter. Find this book at melanienewton.com.

2. If you have been a believer for a while but never really been discipled in the essential truths of the Christian life, we recommend that you work through the *Pathways to a Joyful Walk Bible Study*. It will give you a solid foundation that you can share with others.

3. If you know women who may be Christians but live as though they are nonbelievers, what can you do? Very few churches offer a well-presented course for new believers. If yours does offer such a course, take advantage of that and invite her to take it with you. If your church does not offer this, ask her to meet with you for a few weeks and go through *A Fresh Start Bible Study*.

4. Go to melanienewton.com/disciplemaking to download our "Establish a New or Young Christian" booklet to help you get started in establishing others.

Action steps for ministry leaders

1. Offer a course for new believers in your ministry. Or at least, have some women ready to establish new believers in a one-on-one or small group setting.

2. Go to melanienewton.com/disciplemaking to download our "Establish a New or Young Christian" booklet to give mature Christians encouragement and assistance in establishing new and young believers in your ministry.

3. Some who come to your organized Bible Studies may have been Christians for a while but could be new to Bible study. Provide good tutoring for them. You can see our suggestions in Chapter 8.

Prayer prompts

✓ Ask the Lord to reveal how you might be more intentional in establishing others in their faith.

✓ Ask Him to direct you to one person who needs you to establish her and to give you a desire for her to know the wonderful truths of being in Christ.

✓ If you are the one needing to be discipled, ask Jesus to send someone to establish you in what you need to know.

What others have done

Brenda: "I'm really excited to begin a Bible study with our neighborhood next week. I have two ladies coming and possibly one who is in high school. I am going to really be praying the teenager will join our group. The two ladies coming are very new in their walk with the Lord, and I am thrilled they came to me and want to study God's Word. They were friends I made at the neighborhood book club."

Donna: "I kept hearing you talk about wanting to do a Bible study with your neighbors. So, I decided to try it with mine. We started in January with just a simple 5-lesson study, and five women came. We are starting our second book. This is so exciting!"

Connie: "Just a quick thank you for providing your workshop to our church. It was just the encouragement I needed. I am now sharing the gospel with my friend, an unbeliever, on Wednesday nights and discipling a new believer on Sunday mornings."

CHAPTER 7

Choose to Disciple Others

JESUS FOLLOWERS BECOME DISCIPLEMAKERS

H ow many Bible lessons do you get per week? If you count a Sunday sermon, a weekly women's Bible study class, and your own personal study, that can add up to more than 7 learning sessions per week. How often do you share what you are learning with someone else?

Most of us in Bible-teaching churches have too much inflow without enough overflow. How much can you actually take in without getting overwhelmed and even numb in your response to the word of God? That can lead to restlessness and discontentment. Turn your restlessness into the opportunity for disciplemaking—establishing someone else with the strong roots that you have.

But where do you find those who need what you know? How do you get started? That is what we will discover in this chapter.

RECOGNIZING THE PROBLEM OF INFLOW WITHOUT OVERFLOW

I asked you to consider the number of Bible lessons you get per week. If you count organized teaching or study, that can add up to more than 7 learning sessions per week. Then, consider email devotionals you get or other sources of teaching. Now, you are up to 10 or more. That is a lot of inflow into your brain.

How often do you share what you are learning each week with someone else? I am talking about intentional sharing such as, "I just learned today that…"

Is that sharing more often directed to other mature, educated believers such as those in your women's Bible study group? Or do you share what you are learning from the Lord to younger believers who do not know as much?

The inflow / overflow imbalance

I read this statement several years ago.

We are feeding the 'fed' to death in America. We are into discipling the discipled because it's safer." (Jill Briscoe)

Do you agree or disagree with her?

Many of you have been in Bible studies for years. You have faithfully done those Precept, BSF, CBS, Beth Moore, LifeWay, and Joyful Walk studies. You have a lot of inflow from those studies plus sermons, classes, and small groups swimming around in your head. What do you do with all of that information? How much can you actually take in without getting overwhelmed and even numb in your response to the word of God? It is like that "stuffed" feeling your get after eating the Thanksgiving meal!

The imbalance of too much inflow and not enough overflow is so prevalent in our churches, especially those with strong Bible teaching. And it leads to restlessness and discontentment.

Restlessness is a symptom of forgetting your purpose

It happens over time in large and small Bible studies. Women are excited to study God's Word. But as their knowledge accumulates, the next thing you know they are being snippy about the study questions, whose group they are in, or the table decorations.

The symptoms of too much inflow are evidenced by statements like these:

- "The questions are too easy, not deep enough."

- "We studied that topic two years ago. Why study it again?"

- "I want to be in a group where everyone does their lessons."

Do you recognize any of those statements coming from your own lips?

I have heard them often throughout my years of leading women's Bible studies in churches. I have seen it happen among godly women in very successful Bible studies. I think it is restlessness from too much inflow and not enough overflow. This is evidence that Christian women can get stuck in discipleship—the learning that helps them grow as Jesus followers. We can get so comfortable in "community" that we lose the drive to reach out to others who do not know Jesus yet or do not know Him well. This restlessness is a symptom that we have forgotten our Christ-given commission for disciplemaking.

Now, do not get me wrong. I love Bible study. I have been involved in some fabulous Bible studies over the years, even writing them and lecturing from my detailed study. Women need to know and understand God's Word so they can know their God better and His way of approaching life.

But Jesus told His disciples to go and "make disciples." We are to make disciples as He did. His disciples took in what they learned from Him and shared it with others, taking them through the process of growing in Christ and sharing Him with others. This is called the multiplication process.

Paul described that in 2 Timothy.

*And the things **you have heard me say** in the presence of many witnesses **entrust to reliable people who will** also be qualified to **teach others**. (2 Timothy 2:2)*

Make disciples who make disciples who make disciples.

Do not let all that "inflow" get settled in the recesses of your brain! Let it overflow to someone who needs it. Turn your restlessness into the opportunity for disciplemaking—establishing someone else with the strong roots that you have. But where do you find those who need what you know?

ESTABLISHING THOSE WHO ARE AROUND YOU

Where are the new believers besides anyone you lead to Christ yourself? What about those who have been Christians for a while but have never been discipled to truly know the foundational teachings of how to live as a Christian?

Most likely, new and never-been-discipled Christians are where you are presently connected such as in Bible study groups, in mothers' groups, where you work or live, and at women's events. All you have to do is pay attention and come alongside the one who needs to be discipled.

We have a great example of that in the book of Acts.

Meanwhile a Jew named Apollos, a native of Alexandria, came to Ephesus. He was a learned man, with a thorough knowledge of the Scriptures. He had been instructed in the way of the Lord, and he spoke with great fervor and taught about Jesus accurately, though he knew only the baptism of John. He began to speak boldly in the synagogue. When Priscilla and Aquila *heard him, they **invited him to their home and explained to him the way of God more adequately.** (Acts 18:24-26)*

A married couple, Priscilla and Aquilla, paid attention to a man speaking, recognized that he needed truth, invited him to their home, and discipled him there. Apollos went on to lead many others to Christ and disciple them.

Pay attention

How do you pay attention? Like Priscilla and Aquila did in Acts 18:24-26, pay attention as people talk. Listen to that woman in your small group, the one who is sitting near you at church, or is a newcomer at your women's event. This is meant for any growing Christian to do, not just the group leaders or ministry staff. (If you are leading a Bible study that has several women new to the Bible, we cover how to help them specifically in Chapter 8.)

❖ **Bible study group:** Small groups are fishing pools for disciplemaking. For the one who is new to your Bible study group, do not assume she knows her identity in Christ. She may not be a believer yet. She may be a new believer. When you glance at her study guide, are the spaces mostly blank? She may not know how to read a verse and answer a question. She may be a long-time believer who has never done Bible study before and feels ignorant compared to others. Many Bible studies are written from a certain translation. If her Bible is different, she may not see the same wording used in the questions. SHE NEEDS YOU!

❖ **Newcomer to church or women's event:** As you greet someone who seems to be a newcomer, listen to what she says. Ask her a little about herself. Is she new to your church? Is she new to Bible study? If she is new to attending church or new to reading the Bible for herself, SHE NEEDS YOU!

Several years ago, my daughter and I attended a women's Bible conference at our church. A young woman came to our row and sat by herself not far from us. I invited her to sit next to me. We introduced ourselves and starting getting to know one another throughout the day. My new friend Kathy shared that she was new to the Bible and did not understand much about Christianity. Her son had started attending a Christian school that required parents to read the Bible at night with their child. So, Kathy and her husband were introduced to Christ and the Bible as a result. She was hungry for more. I felt the Lord directing me to take the next step—come alongside in discipling her.

Come alongside in discipling

Come alongside is exactly that. Getting together with someone often, helping them learn truth, and walking with them through applying that truth in their lives. This is where you intentionally connect with the one who needs to be discipled.

Remember those questions I mentioned above coming from women who have had too much inflow of Bible knowledge and not enough overflow? That problem is solved when you become more in tune with the Holy Spirit in the process of disciplemaking.

- "The questions are too easy, not deep enough." Praise God that someone new to the Bible has an opportunity to learn. Invite a neighbor or friend who is new to the Bible so she can learn without being overwhelmed. Do you want "deep study?" Do it on your own. Take advantage of easier studies to disciple someone else in your group who needs you!

- "We studied that topic two years ago. Why study it again?" Life is not always about you. Actually, when you walk with the Lord, it is **never** about you. It is **always about Christ.** Stay Christ-focused and consider how you can help someone else learn the truth from that topic that you have already learned. Invite someone who needs to know that truth and walk beside her in the group.

- "I want to be in a group where everyone does their lessons." Consider why someone does not do the lesson. As I mentioned earlier, she might not know how to do them. Be the one who helps her. Suggest you do them together for fun.

That turns the focus on disciplemaking more than discipleship.

Here is how it would like for various situations:

❖ **Bible study group:** For the one who is new to Bible study and seems to be struggling, ask her if you could get together and work through the lesson. Find a time that works FOR HER and a place that is convenient for her. Work through the lesson together, helping her to find and read the verses then answer the questions. If she is a new Christian, offer to disciple her in the basics of the faith using a basic study designed for new

Christians. I listed what new believers need to know in Chapter 6.

❖ **Newcomer to church or women's event:** If you meet someone who is definitely new to Christ, to church, and likely new to the Bible, get her contact information and invite her to meet you casually within the next week. When you get together, share a little of your story and ask her to share hers. Find out where she is in her walk of faith. Find out what she already knows and what she wants or needs to know.

If she is a new Christian, ask her if you could disciple her to get more established in her faith. Offer to meet with her for a few weeks to help her get a good foundation. Walk through the gospel of Mark with her. Show her how to read the passage and let the Holy Spirit show her something from it. I usually ask the question, "What grabbed your attention?" That is the milk God wants to feed her for that day.

If you like something more structured, choose a basic study guide for new believers such as *A Fresh Start* or another study specifically for new Christians. Arrange your first time together. Work through the new believer's study together the first time. Let her ask you questions. If she wants, she can take it home and work through the next lesson.

That is what I did with Kathy. The next day after the women's conference, I contacted Kathy and invited her to meet me for dinner at a local restaurant during the coming week. When we met together, we talked about her life and her family. She was excited about being a Christian but felt so insecure about everything. I asked if I could disciple her and help her get off to a good start. She agreed. We met for the next 8 weeks, going through *A Fresh Start* together. She loved it! And after we met each week, she shared with her husband all that we learned together. He started growing as a Christian too.

Maybe you already have something that someone used to disciple you when you were a new Christian. Or your church might have discipling materials on hand. Just make sure you walk through the 8 necessary elements of a good foundation that are listed in Chapter 6. [Warning: Cover knowing who Jesus is and what He has done for believers before you cover dealing with sin. Skip around in the book if necessary.]

One of the benefits of discipling someone is that sharing what you know gives you a fuller understanding of what you have. It takes the "inflow" of information to another level. A huge verse from the small book of Philemon grabbed my attention several years ago. It contains a practical truth about the Christian life.

> *I pray that you may* **be active in sharing your faith,** *so that* **you will have a full understanding** *of every good thing we have in Christ. (Philemon 1:6, NIV 1984 version)*

Actively sharing what you know gives you a fuller understanding of what you have. When you have to explain some part of what you have in Christ to someone else in terms that a younger believer can understand, you find out pretty quickly whether you understand it or not. When you can explain it using your own words, that gives you a fuller understanding of the riches you have.

Dear friends, that is LIFESTYLE DISCIPLEMAKING. That is what Jesus is calling you and me to do every day. Come alongside **one** other woman to help her become a better follower of Jesus. This is not creating programs. It is creating a lifestyle and shift in our thinking.

MENTORING: THE "HOW" OF DISCIPLEMAKING

The simplicity of mentoring

Does "pay attention" and "come alongside her" sound like mentoring? Yes, it does. Mentoring is someone older in the Lord helping someone younger in the Lord understand and apply biblical truth to everyday life. It is the **"how"** of discipling and should include all aspects of disciplemaking (one's own spiritual growth as well as connecting with nonbelievers to introduce them to Christ).

Paul gave us examples of what this looks like in 1 Thessalonians.

> *Just as a nursing mother cares for her children, so we cared for you. Because we loved you so much, we were delighted to* **share with you not only the gospel of God but our lives as well.** *... You are witnesses, and so is God, of how holy, righteous and blameless we were among you who believed. For you know that we dealt with each of you as a father deals with his own children,* **encouraging, comforting and urging you to live lives worthy of God,** *who calls you into his kingdom and glory. (1 Thessalonians 2:7-12)*

That is mentoring!

Some call it organic mentoring (non-structured). Really, it is the "ESTABLISH" phase of disciplemaking where someone older in the Lord helps someone younger in the Lord apply biblical truth to everyday life. It is not just for leaders to do. It is for every Christian.

Connecting her with someone else as a mentor

What if the Lord brings a new Christian to your attention, but you know that you will not be able to give her your attention? That is when you connect her with someone else who can build into her life. Paul did that for the Thessalonians.

> We **sent Timothy**, who is our brother and co-worker in God's service in spreading the gospel of Christ, **to strengthen and encourage you in your faith**, (1 Thessalonians 3:2)

Paul could not be there with the new believers so he sent a trusted friend to them. They were not left on their own.

Recently, a new Christian named Sheryl visited a class I was teaching. I invited her to meet me for dinner at a local restaurant where we got acquainted. As we met several times over the next month, I realized that I was not the one who should disciple her. I was already leading four Bible study groups, and I knew that she needed someone else who could give her more personal attention. So, I asked my friend Janet, who loves discipling people one-on-one, if she would pray about discipling Sheryl. The Lord confirmed in Janet's mind and heart that she should do that. Janet discipled Sheryl for several months. Both are loving the experience.

The point is this: If you meet someone who needs to be discipled, take on the challenge yourself or get someone else to do it. SHE NEEDS YOU!

Mentoring is for any Christian

> Therefore **encourage one another** and **build each other up**, just as in fact you are doing. ... And we urge you, brothers and sisters, warn those who are idle and disruptive, **encourage the disheartened**, **help the weak**, be patient with everyone. (1 Thessalonians 5:11, 14)

Those verses were not directed to pastors and church staff but to all the believers in the local church—for anyone at any age or stage of life. You are never too old to have impact for Christ. Encourage. Build up. Help the weak. That is discipling.

Things to remember while mentoring someone

❖ **Make It Stick:** When you explain something, have her repeat it back to you to check her understanding. Do this several times as needed.

❖ **Make It Real:** Adapt what she is learning about her blessings and identity in Christ to real life with her family, friends, and coworkers. For example: When you talk about being loved and accepted unconditionally by God, you could ask her, "How does knowing that help you love your _____ (husband, children, siblings, friends) well?"

❖ **Make Her Responsible:** Encourage her to take responsibility for her own spiritual growth. Have her read the Bible on her own between times when you get together with her.

To follow a "Read through the Bible" plan for regular feeding, lead them to do the New Testament only, always beginning with the gospels. Establishing that relationship with Jesus is top priority. Newborn babies do not need to know all the family history before we establish our love relationship with them.

Talk about prayer being conversation with God that she can do at any time. As you study together, encourage her to obey Jesus in what she is learning. Encourage her to reach out to her peers and share with them what the Lord is doing in her life.

❖ **Stay Christ-Focused:** Christianity is Christ. What they need first and foremost is to get to know Him well and be secure in their relationship with Him. You will not always be there with her, but Jesus will be there. Lead her to recognize Christ as Lord of her life and to be dependent on Him more than on you. In your discussions, always consider what Christ has done for her and wants for her to do in response more than what the culture teaches. Stay Christ-focused.

DISCIPLING ANOTHER PERSON MAKES YOU RELY ON JESUS MORE

Feeling a bit scared or hesitant about discipling a new Christian? Jump right in and do it. Whatever leads you to trust in Jesus more is good for you. If you have not been rooted with this basic information, your discipling experience will be a huge growing experience for you as well.

Give your insecurities to Jesus. He is the one who makes you able to do everything in the Christian life, and that includes discipling a new Christian. You are simply to obey Him and trust His Spirit to work through you. Being scared is a good thing because you will rely on Him more. It is okay to say, *"Lord, I cannot do this on my own, but you can in me and through me. I will trust you with this."* Step out in faith.

STAY CHRIST-FOCUSED & TAKE THE NEXT STEPS

Trust in Jesus to lead you to establish another person. Why not ask the Lord to give you the opportunity to explain forgiveness, redemption, and reconciliation to someone in your sphere of influence this week? It is okay to practice what you would say.

Leave room in your schedule to come alongside an unchurched friend. What might be beneficial for her? When is a good time for her to attend something? Sign up for that and invite her along. Lifestyle disciplemaking focuses outward to help others grow in Christ rather than just focusing on your inward personal growth. Trust Jesus to help you do this. Then, watch what He does!

Jesus invited His followers to go fishing. "Come follow Me, and I will make you fishers of men (and women!)." He took them fishing in their homes (Mark 2), in their churches (Luke 6:6), and in their public places (Luke 5). Where are you fishing?

What if you have a group of women who are new to the Bible? What is the best way to nurture them? That is the subject of the next chapter.

Let Jesus lead you into lifestyle disciplemaking.
Jesus followers become disciplemakers.

TAKE THE LEAP

Thought questions

1. If you have been in Bible studies for years, have you recognized any symptoms of restlessness in yourself as I described in this chapter (complaining that the questions are too easy, you have already done that topic, or wanting to be with people who always

do their lessons)? How do you feel about transferring your focus to helping a less-experienced believer in the group?

2. How many Bible lessons do you get a week? How often do you share what you learn with someone else? How much of that sharing is directed to other mature, educated believers or to younger believers who do not know much?

3. Why is it important to come alongside someone in your group who is struggling or lacking truth in her life rather than assuming she will "catch up" just by being in the group?

4. Where are those new or never-been-discipled believers in your sphere of influence? In what ways do you need to change your thinking about personally discipling them?

5. Is Jesus leading you to disciple someone? Are you ready to do so?

Action steps for individuals

1. If you are in a Bible study group or other small group as a participant:

   - **Pay attention** to those around you. Listen well. Some may be embarrassed by what they do not know so they will not write answers to the questions or speak up in the group.

   - **Come alongside** one who does not know Jesus or know Him well. Invite her somewhere to talk about it. Offer to help her learn how to do a Bible study. Find out what she already knows and what she wants to know. Be willing to walk her through the basics of the faith if she has not been discipled already. Help her catch up with the others in the group.

2. If Jesus is leading you to disciple a young Christian, download the "Establish a New or Young Christian" booklet from my website (melanienewton.com/disciplemaking). This contains information to help you come alongside another person.

Action steps for ministry leaders

1. **If you are a small group leader:** Work through my book *Be a Christ-Focused Small Group Leader*. This resource helps you to lead the mature women in your group to pay attention and come alongside young believers in the group. Share the load of discipling with others.

2. Encourage mature women to be willing to disciple a young Christian. Provide materials for them to use. Make this an important part of your ministry. Download the "Establish a New or Young Christian" booklet from my website (melanienewton.com/disciplemaking). This booklet contains information to help someone pay attention and come alongside another woman.

Prayer prompts

✓ Ask Jesus to show you how to overflow whatever you are learning to someone else who needs to know it.

✓ Trust in Jesus to lead you to establish another person.

✓ Ask Him to give you both willingness and opportunity to be a "Priscilla" to another woman. If you do not feel confident, that is okay because you will depend on Him more. Feel free to say, *"I cannot do this on my own, Lord Jesus, but You can through me."*

What others have done

Michelle: "Our church hosts Pinterest events every month, inviting the community to participate through a Facebook page, Pinterest board, and newspaper ad. We also offer free childcare! The planning team invites the women of our church to be part of the prayer, set up, and childcare teams but NOT to attend the event as a social activity. This strategy makes plenty of room for the unreached. The event is designed with the unreached in mind! As a result, we are drawing between 25 and 30 unchurched women each month ranging in age from young moms to senior adults. We connect with them and follow up in discipleship for any new believers."

Yvette: "Your training encourages and challenges me. It has given us a new vision for our ladies' studies that will help us get out of our comfort zone. We are praying on how and where the Lord is leading us."

Alice: "You can always find one person to disciple. These days, I am a "naptime" disciplemaker because I am at home with two kids under the age of three ... The two girls I am discipling from the nearby university drive to my home while the kids are napping."

CHAPTER 8

Nurture Women Who Are New to the Bible

JESUS FOLLOWERS BECOME DISCIPLEMAKERS

I recently heard a relatively new Christian woman say, "I get lost in our small group Bible study especially when people start throwing out Greek words and what they have learned in other studies. I just want to understand the words that are actually printed here. I feel so ignorant like I can never understand the Bible." My heart just hurt for her. From my experience, I know this precious new-to-the-Bible Christian is not alone in how she feels in our Bible studies. Whether you are a Bible study group leader or just a group member, this chapter will help you properly care for anyone new to the Bible in your group.

When I heard that woman say that she gets lost in our Bible study groups, especially when people start throwing out what they have learned in other studies, my heart hurt for her. She just wanted to understand the words that were actually printed in the biblical text or the current study guide. The experience made her feel ignorant like she could never understand the Bible. From my experience, I know this precious new-to-the-Bible Christian is not alone in how she feels in our Bible studies.

Because I have been listening and watching over the past 25 years of active Bible study leading, I have picked up some insights about nurturing women new to the Bible. The first one is to acknowledge their presence.

ACKNOWLEDGE THEIR PRESENCE

Understanding how "Bible study newbies" feel

Several years ago, I asked women in my Bible study group what they remembered about their first time attending a Bible Study. The descriptions that came back were these: frightened, panicked, lost as a goose, isolated, and crying like a baby. Yet, they did not give up. Some of them kept on because they had signed up for the course and did not want to quit. Others had someone tutor them through the study. One mentioned that only God strengthened her enough to keep trying. Even after two years, one woman said she still gets lost in the regular women's Bible study at her church.

We have women all around us who were not raised in a church setting or do not have years of church life where they were taught from the Bible (sermons, Sunday school classes, other). Or they attended a church that even discouraged personal Bible study. Those are the ones who get lost in our Bible-oriented churches. I call them "Bible study newbies."

If they are new Christians, they need to be discipled in the basics of the faith. We covered the eight necessary elements of a good foundation for them in Chapter 6.

Most first-time attendees to organized Bible Studies are women new to the Bible. They have no clue how to read it to feed themselves. They are like the newborn babies in our own families— hungry for the "milk" of God's Word. Most women's Bible study guides are designed for experienced students. For the "Bible study newbie," working through the study is like trying to chew steak with only a few baby teeth!

We who know the Lord should want to make the experience of those "Bible study newbies" so much better than that. We should not assume that those new-to-the-Bible Christians in a regular Bible study group will catch up just by being there. This lack of nurture can lead to discouragement, insecurity, and a feeling of "I am not smart enough to understand the Bible." Soon, they give up. I have seen this happen. For one sweet woman, I was the guilty one.

When I was the small group leader who assumed

Lynn told us on her first day to our Bible study group that she had never been in a Bible study before this. She was a shy new Christian, having just started attending our church. I thought, "She will catch on as we go through the study each week."

I was wrong, very wrong. Lynn did not know how to read Bible verses and answer questions in a study designed for experienced Bible students. She might get the observation questions, just looking for information. But after that, she would not answer anything. She felt so inadequate.

Instead of coming alongside her, I waited a few weeks. Lynn stopped coming. When I asked why, she told me how hard it was to do the study. I had her moved to a group for beginners, but the whole process of getting to know another group of people was overwhelming. She dropped altogether. I had waited too long to help her. As an experienced follower of Christ, I failed this new Christian.

Since then, I have learned to sympathize with their insecurity and help them get a good start.

SYMPATHIZE WITH THEIR INSECURITY

If a woman is not much of a book learner anyway, she is going to feel insecure right away and even defeated that she will never be able to learn the Bible on her own.

Think about the challenging process of Bible reading and study:

- First, you need a Bible or Bible app. There are so many translations. Where do you start? For someone new to the Bible, recommend she use an easy-to-read translation (NIV, CSB, NLT, ESV) to help her gain confidence in understanding what she is reading.

- Then, you need to know what each part of a Bible verse reference means—book, chapter, and verse. The Bible is one book containing a collection of 66 books combined together for our benefit. It is divided into two main parts: Old Testament and New Testament. Someone new to the Bible needs to know that Bibles and Bible apps have a table of contents to help find each book in the Bible.

- Once you find the verse reference, someone new to the Bible needs to be able to read it and usually repeat back what it says in answer to a question in the study guide. Most Bible studies are written using a specific translation. If she is not using the same translation, the question might not use the wording in the verse reference. That creates confusion as well.

I attended my first Bible study with my college roommate. Because I did not know much other than Psalm 100 (memorized during Vacation Bible School) and Luke 2 (the Christmas story), I felt pretty nervous. I brought the Bible I had been given as a child. My leader helped me find the right place to read and showed me how to discover truth from a Bible verse. She prayed for God to help me understand it. I was so amazed at the treasure I discovered that I could not wait to get back the next week to learn more. That small group Bible study literally changed my life!

Come alongside that woman who is new to the Bible and let her know you want to help her as much as you can. Show compassion to the woman who signs up to attend your Bible study and then feels absolutely overwhelmed because it is too hard for her. Help her. SHE NEEDS YOU.

PROVIDE THE BEST TUTORING FOR THEM

Anyone can study the Bible for themselves. That is truth that everyone needs to know—from beginner through any experience level. The Bible is God's Word for every one of us whether you are a book learner or not. The Holy Spirit will help you understand what you are reading. That is what God desires for you so He makes sure you are enabled to do it.

I love this verse from 1 Corinthians.

*What we have received is not the spirit of the world, but **the Spirit** who is from God, **so that we may understand what God has freely given us**. (1 Corinthians 2:12)*

Our God wants us to know and understand what He has freely given us. You can ask the Lord to teach you through what you are reading in His Word. That is a promise and His will. He will answer that prayer with, "Yes!" Be ready yourself to explain to a new believer what she has in Christ. We included this in Chapter 6.

Twenty years ago, I was in a large Bible study with about 200 women. One of the women came up to us leaders and said, "My mom would like to come to this Bible Study. But she does not know anything about the Bible. Do you think you could offer a beginners' group?" DUH! Why had we never thought of this before?!

The next fall we offered a small group for "Bible study beginners" as part of our large study. Within a couple of weeks, we had fifteen women signed up for it! There was a genuine need we had not previously acknowledged. So, we asked two women to be the group leaders whose hearts wanted to help those beginners at Bible study.

The leaders gave their "newbies" book tabs for their Bibles (today, showing how to use a Bible app). They selected specific questions from the lesson for the women to work through in the group and a few to work through at home (so not to be overwhelmed by the whole study). They helped them learn how to read a question, look up a verse, and try to answer the question afterward. They worked at explaining things in basic terms, making it easier for those women to understand.

Several of those women grew like weeds in their faith and in their Bible study skills. In three to four years, they were leading Bible study small groups of their own. It was fantastic!

The example I shared above is an example of intentional tutoring for Bible study beginners in a regular study designed for experienced Christians. You can also work through the weekly Bible study lesson with someone in your group who is new to the Bible until she feels comfortable doing it on her own.

What is even better is offering a Bible study designed especially for women new to the Bible.

CHOOSE A SHORT AND EASY STUDY FOR WOMEN NEW TO THE BIBLE

Whether you are leading a group of women who are new to the Bible or just doing a one-on-one study, choose a study that makes it easier for them to learn. That is the whole premise behind our short and easy *Graceful Beginnings* books for women new to the Bible.

The *Graceful Beginnings* lessons are basic with simple terms and easy-to-understand questions. Any woman can work through one of these studies and feel confident as she learns something from God's Word in each lesson. We hope she will be ready to pick up another study and keep going. Our goal is that she gets to know both God and His Word better with each lesson. Any "Bible study newbie" will learn how to study the Bible with confidence and joy!

Since the *Graceful Beginnings* lessons are designed for anyone new to the Bible, you will probably want to work through the first book together with the other person or small group as an example of how to do a Bible study. If you are discipling a new Christian, start with *A Fresh Start*. The other books can be done in any order.

In a one-on-one setting:

You can help a "Bible study newbie" by doing a Bible study book designed for beginners with her one-on-one. This is really beneficial to do before she signs up for the large group study. It is much less intimidating to someone just learning from the Bible. The following process is based on the format of our *Graceful Beginnings* studies.

- **Start with prayer:** Ask the Lord Jesus to teach both of you what He wants you to learn through the lesson.

- **Work through** the lesson together when you meet. Allow an hour.

- **Look up and read each Bible verse.** That way you can make sure she knows how to find Bible verses to read and how to answer the question asked about that verse.

- **Read the summary paragraphs** and discuss anything confusing or interesting.

- **Encourage her to listen to any associated podcasts** before you meet. Ask what grabbed her attention and highlight specific things you want her to know. Always discuss the application question at the end.

- **Encourage her to do any extra Bible reading and reflecting on her own** before the next time you meet. Talk about what she learned in her reading and reflecting from the last lesson before you work through the next lesson.

In a group setting:

It is helpful to have each woman work through the lessons on her own before meeting together to discuss them. If they do this, the lessons should take an hour or less to cover. This could easily fit into a workplace setting to use your lunch break for disciplemaking. See Chapter 11 for ideas to do this.

The process of leading the lesson is similar to the one-on-one time mentioned above but faster since the women have already had a chance to consider their answers.

- Start with prayer.

- **Look up and read each Bible verse.** Let them read the questions and answer them.

- **Read the summary paragraphs** and discuss anything confusing or interesting.

- **Encourage them to listen to any associated podcasts** before you meet. Ask what grabbed their attention and highlight specific things you want them to know. Always discuss the application question at the end.

There you go. Enjoy the blessings of discovering God's Word together with women who are new to the Bible. Watch her experience a joyful walk with Jesus. The bottom line is this: Make it easy for women new to the Bible to learn and not give up!

Ask Jesus to help you with all of the above steps to choosing a Bible study for yourself or for your group. Depend on Him to show you what to do. He is faithful!

STAY CHRIST-FOCUSED & TAKE THE NEXT STEPS

For all of you women who have influence over other women in your church, women's ministry, or any kind of small group, let us change the way we feed our Christian sisters who are new to the Bible. Trust Jesus to help you do this. Then, watch what He does!

As women trust in Christ and grow in their faith, the next phase of disciplemaking is to LAUNCH them to do all of that with their peers. We will cover what the launch phase looks like in the next chapter.

Let Jesus lead you into lifestyle disciplemaking. Jesus followers become disciplemakers.

TAKE THE LEAP

Thought questions

1. Do you remember what it was like when you were new to the Bible? How did you feel?

2. Have you noticed women who are new to the Bible in your group? What did anyone do to help them find verses and answer questions?

Action steps for individuals

1. Are you in a small group and recognize someone new to the Bible? Come alongside her and offer to help her learn how to work through a lesson. Work through 2-3 lessons together until you know she understands the process. Stay close through the rest of the study, talking about each lesson before the group meets. Keep confirming what she is discovering as she answers the questions. Let your small group leader know that you are helping her.

2. Consider the women in your workplace. Some are nonbelievers. But many coworkers are women who may be Christians with

some church background but are still new to the Bible. Offer a Bible study at work during lunch. We give more help for this in Chapter 11.

3. If you have several friends who are new to the Bible, consider asking them to do a *Graceful Beginnings* study with you. Use the suggestions I have given above for leading the group. Most of the studies also have a suggested discussion guide as well.

4. If you are a Christian who is new to the Bible, please ask an experienced Christian to help you learn how to study the Bible for yourself. The Spirit of God inside you will make you able to understand God's Word over time. And it will be so satisfying. You will not be hungry again.

Action steps for ministry leaders

Women who are unfamiliar with the Bible attend your church, your Bible study, and your women's group. You may not know who they are, but they are there.

1. Consider offering a "Beginners" group for those new to the Bible. Ask the Lord for leaders who will nurture them well.

2. Keep a supply of Bible studies for beginners on hand to help your new women get a great start in studying the Bible.

3. **Are you a small group leader?** Assume that some of the women in your small group do not know how to find a Bible verse, read it, and answer a question. Explain churchy words the first time you use them (Gentiles, grace, salvation, redemption) and repeat until you think everyone has heard. If you are studying the gospels and talk about John, say which John it is— John the Baptist or John the disciple of Jesus. Try to find someone to come alongside a Bible study newbie in the group at the beginning of the study so she will not become discouraged. Do not assume she will catch on by being in the group.

4. **Are you a ministry director?** Do everything you can to communicate to women that you want to provide a safe place for women who are new to the Bible at your church. Offer them a group for beginners. Or pair them with someone who can help them work through their lesson in your regular Bible studies.

Prayer prompts

✓ Ask Jesus to give you compassion for anyone new to the Bible and the willingness to help them learn how to feed themselves from His Word.

✓ Ask Him to show you the women in your group whom He wants you to disciple in particular. Trust Him to lead you to those who need your help and the courage to approach them.

✓ Ask Him to lead the mature Christians in your group to join in discipling the younger Christians.

✓ Submit yourself to the Lord to be a disciplemaker for Him. Praise Him for the privilege of joining Him in His work.

What others have done

Melanie: I asked Janet to disciple Sheryl, who is a new Christian and new to the Bible. They are going through one of the Graceful Beginnings books together. From Sheryl: "Thank you for hooking me up with Janet. You have both been a blessing." From Janet: "Sheryl and I are doing well. We are about halfway through the book *Painting the Portrait of Jesus*. She asks questions and is understanding the material. It has been fun to get to know her."

Lindsey: "I had the idea of finding other women from my church who work in the same area of the city as I do. I found a few, invited them to join me for lunch once a month at a convenient restaurant to their workplaces, and said to bring friends. The lunches are short, informal, and good for building relationships—a creative idea for working women who have very little free time to get together with other women. I found this to be a great place to invite unchurched coworkers."

Launch Disciples to Make More Disciples

CHAPTER 9

Multiply Impact Beyond Yourself

JESUS FOLLOWERS BECOME DISCIPLEMAKERS

Most church ministries do a pretty good job at discipleship through teaching. We are weakest at encouraging and preparing women to intentionally build relationships with unchurched women and share about Christ in casual conversation as opportunity arises. In other words, local churches are okay at establishing Christians but not-so-good at launching them to do the work of ministry apart from the church.

Have you been trained and encouraged to start a Bible study apart from your church? As you have read through this book, I hope you have seen ways to be a disciplemaker while growing in your faith. Remember that a disciplemaker is one who makes disciples that make disciples. The goal is not just to teach but also to train others to continue the process. We described that in Chapter 1 as the LAUNCH phase of lifestyle disciplemaking. It goes beyond just growing in your own faith. It is launching out to reach your peers.

> **Disciplemaking** is seeing people trust in Christ and grow in Him while **at the same time** equipping them to go back and help others repeat this process. Disciplemaking is outward-focused.

This is the process: You trust in Christ, choose to follow Him, and grow in your faith (discipleship) **while at the same time** you learn how to reach new people for Christ, build them up in the faith, and help them reach their peers (disciplemaking). Discipleship is incomplete without disciplemaking.

Jesus did not leave the option open for us to focus only on ourselves. And He trained His followers to make disciples then **launched** them to do so using what they learned from Him.

THE EXAMPLE OF JESUS

The training phase

Jesus challenged His followers to become "fishers of people."

> *"Come, follow me," Jesus said, "and I will send you out to fish for people." (Mark 1:17)*

He spent His second and third year of ministry preparing them to connect with nonbelievers and to establish believers in their faith.

Reading the gospels, you will see Jesus preparing His followers to teach the gospel message, to have compassion on people and meet their needs, and to interact with both the faithful and the skeptics.

As Jesus traveled with His followers, He let them take part in His ministry to prepare them for their own work. They watched Him connect with different kinds of people—locals, foreigners, preachers, prostitutes, poor, rich, distraught parents, and others. Then, He began to launch them into ministry for themselves.

The launch phase

I like that word "launch." According to the Oxford Dictionary online, the definition of launch as a verb includes these aspects:

- to set (a boat) in motion by pushing it or allowing it to roll into the water, or
- to start or set in motion (an activity or enterprise)

Since we know that four of the disciples were fishermen, the first definition fits well. They were the boat being pushed by Jesus. But the second definition fits better with what Jesus spent His time doing. In His training, He prepared them so that He could release them to start something new—making disciples for Him.

Let us look at what He did while He was alive on earth.

> *When Jesus had called the Twelve together, he gave them power and authority to drive out all demons and to cure diseases, and **he sent them out to proclaim the kingdom of God and to heal the sick. ...** If people do not welcome you, leave their town and shake the dust off your feet as a testimony against them." **So they set out and went from village to village, proclaiming the good news and healing people***

*everywhere. ... When the **apostles returned, they reported to Jesus what they had done.** Then he took them with him and they withdrew by themselves to a town called Bethsaida, (Luke 9:1-2, 5-6, 10)*

Jesus sent them out as a group to take the gospel to nearby towns and practice what they learned from Him. They did what He told them to do then reported back to Him what they had done.

*After this the Lord appointed seventy-two others and **sent them two by two** ahead of him to every town and place where he was about to go. He told them, "The harvest is plentiful, but the workers are few. Ask the Lord of the harvest, therefore, to send out workers into his harvest field." ... "Whoever listens to you listens to me; whoever rejects you rejects me; but whoever rejects me rejects him who sent me." **The seventy-two returned with joy** ... (Luke 10:1-2, 16-17)*

Jesus expanded His ministry beyond Himself and the twelve Apostles by sending out seventy disciples to take the gospel message to nearby towns to prepare for His arrival in those same towns. Notice that He sent them out in pairs. Our Lord knows we need encouragement and support from other believers as we connect with people who do not already know Him.

After His death and resurrection, Jesus met with His followers and launched them out to do the work of making disciples who make disciples. He turned His ministry over to those He had trained.

*Then Jesus came to them and said, "All authority in heaven and on earth has been given to me. Therefore **go and make disciples** of all nations, baptizing them in the name of the Father and of the Son and of the Holy Spirit, and **teaching them to obey everything I have commanded you.** And surely I am with you always, to the very end of the age." (Matthew 28:18-20)*

Jesus followers would not be alone, relying on their own power to do what Jesus commissioned them to do.

*But you **will receive power when the Holy Spirit comes on you**; and **you will be my witnesses** in Jerusalem, and in all Judea and Samaria, and to the ends of the earth. (Acts 1:8)*

105

Jesus followers were prepared and launched to be disciplemakers. This multiplication of disciplemakers has continued through the years to the one who shared the good news with you.

LAUNCHING DISCIPLEMAKERS TODAY

From all the disciplemaking trainings I have done in recent years and visiting with many women church leaders, I have concluded two things about most Bible-teaching churches:

- We do a pretty good job of teaching Christians once they become believers and start attending our churches. Praise God for that!

- We are weakest at encouraging and preparing women to intentionally build relationships with women who are unchurched. And we are weak at training women to share their faith in casual conversation when they are given the opportunity to do so.

In other words, local churches may be good at establishing Christians but not-so-good at launching them to do the work of ministry apart from the church. As you have read through the chapters in this book so far, I hope you have seen ways to be a disciplemaker while growing in your faith.

Let us look at how to launch disciplemakers from an individual perspective and from a church ministry perspective.

Launching as individuals:

Are you discipling a new or young believer to help her get established in her faith? Then, also teach her how to connect with her peers to share her new faith with them. Another option is to invite a friend to do this with you. Both ways are multiplying disciplemakers for Jesus. See all the tools we shared with you in previous chapters:

- *Chapter 2:* Pray and Love

- *Chapter 4:* Prepare a 3-Word Faith Story and a 5-Minute Faith Story

- *Chapter 5:* Practice Conversation Transitions and Sharing the Gospel Facts

All of these are included in the "Prepare to Share" booklet we offer to you in our "Lifestyle Disciplemaking Resources" at the end of this book.

Then, you can help her establish a new believer. Whenever someone she knows trusts in Christ, she can disciple her friend with the same resources you used to establish her. That is why having a prepared Bible study guide such as *A Fresh Start Bible Study* is so beneficial. It becomes easily transferrable.

You could also establish the new believer together—first, with you helping her then with you watching her and supporting her while she does it. That is the coaching method: you watch what I do, you do it with me, you do it while I watch, and you do it on your own. Train women in your sphere of influence to connect with and establish others.

The next phase is to actually release them to pursue disciplemaking as a lifestyle, individually applied. We are not called to do ministry exactly the same way. One may be great at one-on-one teaching. Another might be a wonderful small group leader. Some might be effective engagers at church events or serve well in the local community. We need to encourage one another to pursue ministry the way Jesus has designed for each of us to do. That is how Jesus' ministry multiplies.

Lifestyle disciplemaking works best out in the world away from the church building. That means individuals are doing it in their daily lives. You can be a part of that multiplication of disciplemakers as you train women within your sphere of influence to connect with nonbelievers and establish believers on their own.

Launching from women's ministry or other church ministry:

The same tools mentioned above for connecting with nonbelievers work well in a church ministry setting where there is training and support to actually use them. Continual encouragement and easily accessible tools are very important to instill a lifestyle of disciplemaking in the women of your church.

> An effective ministry is not necessarily a big or busy ministry, but one that is regularly reaching new people for Christ, building them up in the faith and **equipping them to reach their generation** for Christ. (Sonlife Ministries, "Growing Healthy Women in Ministry")

The goal of any ministry is not just to produce disciples but to grow disciplemakers for Jesus. That means you are not to just teach but also to train.

If you are a ministry leader at your church, we give you suggestions in the "Action steps for ministry leaders" at the end of this chapter.

For more help to incorporate disciplemaking into your women's ministry, see Chapter 12, "Transition to a Disciplemaking-Focused Women's Ministry." We give you help in that chapter to transition your existing women's ministry toward disciplemaking—not as a program but to make disciplemaking part of the everyday life of women in your church.

STAY CHRIST-FOCUSED & TAKE THE NEXT STEPS

By faith, you can be a disciplemaker as Jesus commissioned you to be. You can do this in your personal life and small group ministry. Disciplemaking is a lifestyle, not a program. It is investing your life in your two-fold purpose as a believer in Christ.

You can be a disciplemaker at any age or stage of life. Someone around you needs to know Jesus or needs to know Him better. And you can be confident that whatever Jesus calls you to do, He empowers you to do through His Spirit.

You are commissioned by the Lord Jesus to make disciples. Through this book, we have prepared you to do so as Jesus prepared His own disciples. The next step is to choose lifestyle disciplemaking and depend on the Holy Spirit to give you opportunity to lead others to Christ.

> Jesus Christ calls us to a new life, clothes us with himself, commissions us with a purpose, and empowers us to fulfill that purpose—to follow Him as His disciples and to live for Him as disciplemakers.

Trust Jesus to help you do this. Say "yes" and jump in with both feet! Then, watch what He does!

One specific way to jump in with both feet is to start and lead a Bible study that is outside of your church ministry structure. The next chapter will give ideas to help you do that.

Let Jesus lead you into lifestyle disciplemaking.
Jesus followers become disciplemakers.

TAKE THE LEAP

Thought questions

1. If you have had training in the "how-to's" of ministry, consider what benefited you the most that you could share with those new to ministry. Be willing to share that with someone just starting out.

2. Have you discipled someone who has discipled someone else? How did that work out? What did both of you learn in the process?

3. Look at the verses in this chapter to see how Jesus trained His disciples and launched them into ministry. He will do the same for you.

4. Have you asked Jesus to show you how you can best use your gifts in disciplemaking? Why not ask Him today?

Action steps for individuals

1. Encourage anyone you are discipling to reach out to their peers. Do the preparation work together using the tools we suggest in CONNECT Chapters 2 through 5: identifying nonbelievers, praying for them and interacting with them, practicing their faith story and conversation transitions, and learning the gospel facts. These are all available as worksheets in our "Prepare to Share" booklet available at melanienewton.com/disciplemaking.

2. Invite a friend to connect with nonbelievers around you. Do the preparation work together using the worksheets we provide in our "Prepare to Share" booklet.

3. Start and lead a Bible study group outside of church. This is a great way to practice the inflow / overflow of accumulated Bible knowledge. We will cover how to do this in the next chapter.

4. Be willing to establish a younger believer who is in your Bible study small group at church. Reach out to her without being asked. Let your leaders know and keep them informed.

Action steps for ministry leaders

1. Provide transferable resources and methods for women to CONNECT with nonbelievers.

   - Pass out worksheets for preparing your faith stories. Schedule a faith story sharing time so women are prepared. It is always uplifting to see how creative our God is when it comes to drawing us to Him.

   - Pass out gospel facts sheets for them to choose one to learn. Host a gospel sharing training with role-playing. Pair two women together to share the gospel with each other in a relaxed conversational style.

   - Recruit and train designated engagers for your next women's event where newcomers might be present.

   - Offer women's gatherings at different days and times, not just Tuesday nights or Saturday mornings. Brainstorm how to draw in those who feel left out of existing church ministries. Ask for input from women who are not involved or do not attend. "What would draw you to attend something? What would make you feel welcome and want to come?"

2. Provide transferable resources and methods for women to ESTABLISH new and young believers.

   - Provide follow-up materials to use with new believers and Bible studies for beginners. See Chapters 7 and 8 for suggestions. Keep them on hand and make them readily available for women to use in discipling others. For resources, we suggest using our short and easy *Graceful Beginnings* studies which are self-contained and do not require showing videos or reading additional leader notes.

   - Offer a "beginners' study" for anyone new to the Bible. Have a few mature women leading it who can disciple those who attend.

3. **Practice the inflow/overflow principle.** Women turned on to Jesus and introduced to Bible study want to soak up the learning. That is a natural tendency. They may feel inadequate to teach someone else. You need to intentionally communicate to maturing Christians their commission to teach others. Help women to trust in Jesus for the ability to teach someone else. He

is the one who makes each one of us able to do what He calls us to do. We need to be obedient and dependent on Him.

4. **Give inexperienced women opportunity to teach and disciple within women's ministry.** Encourage a culture of permission and trust where people feel the freedom to use their individual giftedness, to try leading, and to fail so they can learn from that. Pair them with an experienced leader. Jesus allowed question and answer sessions about His own teaching (Mark 4:10; 9:11, 28-29; 10:10) and took His disciples aside to talk about their ministry experiences (Luke 9:10; 10:17). He taught them how to handle opposition to their teaching (Mark 11:27-33; 12:13-17). He coached them as they were doing the work. You can coach women new to ministry as well by doing the same things Jesus did.

5. **Train small group leaders for discipling and disciplemaking.** Since small groups are fishing pools for young Christians, this is a great place to incorporate disciplemaking and encourage it among the mature women who attend—participants as well as leaders. Our book *Be a Christ-Focused Small Group Leader* has a section on disciplemaking in a small group.

Prayer prompts

✓ Ask Jesus to lead you to what He wants you to do to launch out beyond your church to reach and train others to follow Him.

✓ Ask Jesus to help you be part of the multiplication process of disciplemaking by launching those you have been teaching or training into reaching their peers for Christ.

What others have done

Debbie: "I have been in a neighborhood Bunco group for several years, praying for God to open up a way to share Christ with the women. This summer, I invited my neighbors to get together with me one night a week and just read through the book of Mark--a few verses at a time. The women come from backgrounds ranging from no faith to lots of Bible knowledge. We focus on what we are reading together so each woman can contribute. No study guide or homework to do other than reading some verses during the week and reflecting on them. Several are coming and bringing their questions."

CHAPTER 10

Start and Lead a Bible Study Group

JESUS FOLLOWERS BECOME DISCIPLEMAKERS

D o you want to do a Bible study and would rather do it in a community with other women rather than by yourself? Maybe you have been thinking about starting a Bible study and inviting others to join you but you do not know where to start. Are you afraid that you do not know enough of the Bible to lead a Bible study for a group? Does the thought of directing a discussion make your knees tremble?

Did you know that everyone feels inadequate when they start out? You are not alone. I have been where you are. Thankfully, Jesus took me beyond my insecurities. He will do the same for you. You can step out in faith and just do it. I am here to help you and be your cheerleader through the process. In this chapter, I will give you suggestions on how to launch a Bible study group as part of lifestyle disciplemaking.

HOW IT BEGAN FOR ME

I remember being a young Christian woman who was just learning how to dive into the Bible and find all its treasures. I was learning so much about Jesus that I wanted to share that learning experience with others. But I did not know how.

At first, I tried a few small study guides and just basically read through them with a group of friends. After college, I joined an organized women's Bible Study where the discussion leaders had us go around the circle reading and answering the questions. I knew there had to be a better way.

Fast forward a few years. Our family was led by the Lord to a new church with a weekly women's Bible study. The group leaders wrote the study guides we used so they were invested in them. I saw the enthusiasm. The leaders met together to share their own answers and what they were learning on their own from the study. They carried that enthusiasm to the small group discussion. This was full of joy—and fun!

They asked me to be a part of that ministry, and that is where it took off for me! Many of the Bible study guides on my website came directly from that ministry, which was appropriately called JOY Bible Study.

My joyful walk with Jesus was stimulated by watching other joy-filled women lead the Bible study discussion. I learned that I could do it too. I was able to step above my insecurities and learn how to lead a Bible study discussion with joy and confidence. That so changed my life! Joyful Walk Ministries was born during that time.

Many churches offer weekly Bible studies for women. All you have to do is sign up. But a lot of churches do not offer Bible studies for women because the churches are too small or have no one to lead the way. Starting and leading a Bible study group outside of your church ministry structure is part of the launch phase of lifestyle disciplemaking. If Jesus is leading you to start a Bible study group, here are some suggestions to help you get started.

START AND LEAD BY FAITH

You can start a Bible study group by faith

Followers of Jesus Christ are to live every day by faith. That is what Paul is communicating to us in Galatians.

> *I have been crucified with Christ and **I no longer live, but Christ lives in me.** The life I now live in the body, **I live by faith** in the Son of God, who loved me and gave Himself for me. (Galatians 2:20)*

The life you and I live every day is by faith in the Son of God—Jesus Himself. Christ not only lives in you, He is living through you. If you are being prompted by the Lord to start a Bible study, just say, *"Yes, I will do this, Lord. Please help me."* Jesus is with you every step of the way and in every situation—in your church, neighborhood, community, or workplace. At any age or stage of life, someone around you needs to know Jesus or to know Him better through studying the Bible.

Faith means you step out in a direction of trusting Jesus to get you through whatever it is you are doing. It leads to becoming a God-dependent woman. And whatever makes you depend upon God more is good for you!

You can start and lead a Bible study group not because you are so great or smart or have been a Christian a long time or know the Bible really well. You can do this because Jesus is the one who enables you to do it.

You can lead a Bible study without knowing all the answers.

No one knows all the answers anyway! Just delete that insecurity from your mind. You do not need a seminary degree to lead a Bible study for others, just a teachable heart and mind. Ask Jesus to teach you what you need to know for your group. Being the leader presses you to grow and learn for yourself. Whether you have been studying the Bible for two years or doing it for decades, share what you know and what you are learning as you lead others to do the same. It is a win-win!

This is a good way to put into practice the "Inflow / Overflow Principle." I mentioned in Chapter 7 that there is a problem of too much inflow and not enough outflow in many of our Bible-teaching churches. You may have been in Bible studies for years and have a lot of inflow from those studies plus sermons, classes, and small groups swimming around in your head. What do you do with all of that information so that you do not feel overwhelmed and even numb in your response to the word of God? The best way is to start and lead a Bible study with women who need to know what you have learned. You will also benefit from it.

You can lead a Bible study group even if you are scared

Give your insecurities to Jesus. He is the one who makes you able to do everything in the Christian life, and that includes starting a Bible study group. You are simply to obey Him and trust His Spirit to work through you. Being scared is a good thing because you will rely on Him more.

It is okay to say, *"Lord, I cannot do this on my own, but you can in me and through me. I will trust you with this."* Then, watch what He does!

Desire the benefits of starting and leading a Bible study group

Starting and leading a Bible study group can be one of the greatest adventures you have ever tried. And it is good for you.

- Leading a Bible study group **presses you to grow** and learn for yourself. You always learn more when you prepare to help someone else grow in their faith.

- Leading a Bible study group also teaches you how **to depend on Jesus Christ more**. And whatever leads you to depend on Him is a good thing for you. We are to live by faith in Him and let Him live His life through us.

Say "yes" and leap into this adventure with both feet.

GETTING STARTED

Start with prayer

Talk it over with Jesus. Let Him know of your desire to start a Bible study group. Ask Him to help you discern what you should study and to show you whom you should ask to join you.

Consider whom to invite

Consider ways to invite women to join you for a study. This is easier now with available social media platforms and email. You can personally invite neighbors, coworkers, or church friends. Or you can put an invitation on Facebook or another social media platform and see who responds.

Decide when to meet

You can meet at any time that works for you and your group—early in the morning before school or work, in the evening, or on Saturday mornings. You could offer a lunch-and-learn Bible study for your coworkers (see Chapter 11). Whatever works for you and for those you invite. Go for it.

It does not have to be every week. I know of several groups of friends who meet only twice a month for Bible study. It does help to not go too long between meetings, though. You can lose consistency in thought if too much time passes. At least, I do!

Decide where to meet

Meeting in someone's home is usually nice, but it does not always work. Outside of homes, the possibilities are endless. Restaurants can be noisy, making it hard to hear one another. But some have side rooms you can reserve. Meeting at a room in your church might be the most convenient place, especially if you like to know you will always have a place to meet away from crowds! But that depends on the openness of your church to have outside groups using the building. Remember that you want everyone to be able to hear and see each other. And you can meet online through Zoom, FaceTime, or other online platforms.

Start with something for the first time. Then, you can try different days, times, and places until you find something that works well for your group.

Select a Bible study guide that interests you

Your passion about the study will be infectious to your group. If you are excited about doing a certain study, it will be easier to get others interested.

❖ **If this is your first time to lead a study:** We recommend that you choose a Bible study guide that is short and easy to lead. If you have some women in your group who are new to the Bible, you want lessons that are simple and easy-to-understand for beginners. Our *Graceful Beginnings* short and easy studies work well for beginners, fit well in a limited discussion time of an hour or less, and are easy to lead.

❖ **If you already have experience leading a Bible study small group:** You may want to choose a study designed for growing Christians who already have some experience studying the Bible. You can tell this by the length of the lessons and whether the questions assume you have a working knowledge of the Bible.

You can visit the "Free Bible Studies for Women" page on my website to see what is available there. We also have links to other pages that offer Bible studies for women that you can download and see if they might work for you.

All of the above information and more is available in the "Start and Lead a Bible Study Group" booklet on our "Disciplemaking" page. The booklet also includes a detailed section on choosing a Bible study guide for your group.

Set a start date

Set a start date, notify those you are inviting, and tell them how to get the study materials. You could order books for all the group members to have on hand the first time you meet. Or you can give the link for each group member to order her own book. Whatever works best for you.

LEADING THE GROUP

There are two roles of a Bible study group leader. You begin both of those roles the first time you get together.

❖ **Role #1: Content Guardian** (guarding how the truth from God's Word is presented and received). As Content Guardian for your group, you have authority to control the content of the Bible study discussion.

❖ **Role #2: Community Builder** (built around shared study and application of God's Word). As Community Builder for your group, you manage the group interaction to help them love one another well.

Doing these roles effectively leads to a healthy group.

Prepare wisely as "Content Guardian"

Preparation is very important as you lead any kind of Bible study group. Always start with prayer for Jesus to help you learn what He wants you to know from the lesson. Then, you diligently work through the lesson yourself and review what you have done to make a plan for leading the lesson. As the Content Guardian for the group, you have the authority to determine what your group will cover. Practice speaking through your plan, asking the Lord to show you what your group needs to learn.

You can download our "Start and Lead a Bible Study Group" booklet which includes what to do on the first day your group meets, how to prepare as you do your lesson, and how to lead the discussion using a study guide with or without accompanying videos. It also includes helpful suggestions to lead a Bible study without using a study guide.

Lead graciously as "Community Builder" through challenging situations

Approach your roles with humility and grace as you guide your group members through reading the living, transforming Word of God together. Keep your group focused on Christ and His work in their lives throughout the discussion. Ask Jesus to help you do this in a way that pleases Him and shows love to the women. When you stay focused on Christ and dependent on Him, He will guide you in your roles as Content Guardian and Community Builder.

As you read through the Scriptures and work through the questions according to your plan, challenging situations will happen in every group. Some group members will not work on their lessons before the meeting. You will need to manage talkative people so they do not dominate the discussion while affirming the quieter ones to share their answers. You will need to interrupt any attempt from the group members to "fix" each other's problems. You must point them to Jesus instead. There will be moments when you need to decide whether to clarify the truth if a comment needs further explanation or just let it go. Avoid getting bogged down on any one issue. Be ready to give emotional support if the discussion causes someone to cry.

Our "Start and Lead a Bible Study Group" booklet includes more detailed guidance to help you lead graciously through these and other challenging situations.

May Jesus make your time as a Bible study leader very fruitful for Him. Enjoy the blessings of discovering God's Word together with a group of people and watch each one experience a joyful walk with Jesus. It will be a great adventure!

STAY CHRIST-FOCUSED & TAKE THE NEXT STEPS

Step out in faith and just do it! Ask Jesus to help you with all of the above steps to start and lead a Bible study group. Depend on Him to show you what to do. He is faithful! See what He does as you trust Him with this decision. Go ahead, launch out onto the adventure! Then, watch what He does!

One specific way to launch into the adventure is in your workplace. The next chapter will give ideas to use your lunch break for disciplemaking.

Let Jesus lead you into lifestyle disciplemaking.
Jesus followers become disciplemakers.

TAKE THE LEAP

Thought questions

1. What are your insecurities and concerns about leading a Bible study if you have not done it before? Give them to Jesus and say, *"Yes, Lord. I will trust you with these."* Then, watch what He does! Go ahead, begin the adventure.

2. If you are leading (or have led) a Bible study for a group in your church, what do you think your biggest challenges will be in starting and leading a study outside of the church?

Action steps for individuals

1. Consider starting and leading a Bible study in your neighborhood, family, workplace, or group of friends. You can download our "Start and Lead a Bible Study" booklet with step-by-step instructions to get you moving forward to do this.

2. If you want more help for leading a small group, read our leader's handbook, *Be a Christ-Focused Small Group Leader.* You can get this from my website and most online bookstores.

Action steps for ministry leaders

1. Intentionally invite women to start and lead Bible Studies outside of church. Provide leader training for them and suggested resources to use.

2. For leader training, we recommend you use the handbook, *Be a Christ-Focused Small Group Leader.* It applies to leading a group anywhere, not just in a church setting.

3. Invite those who are leading a Bible study or small group outside of women's ministry to any training and encouragement gatherings you offer to those who are leading your own small groups. This will send the message that what they are doing is just as important as what those within the church are doing. And this will encourage others to launch out and start Bible studies outside of the church because they know they will not be alone.

Prayer prompts

- ✓ Give your insecurities about leading a group to the Lord Jesus.
- ✓ Ask Jesus to teach you what you need to know for your group.
- ✓ Ask Him for wisdom in how to manage the marvelously varied women in your group.
- ✓ Ask Him to build community among them that is focused on Him more than on you.
- ✓ Ask Jesus to help you respond graciously to any challenge. Depend on Him to show you what to do. He is faithful!
- ✓ Pray for yourself to stay Christ-focused and Christ-dependent as a leader.

What others have done

Marilyn: "I began learning the Bible by reading with a high school friend, then at the Baptist Student Union at college, then I was discipled one-on-one by an older lady. After several years, I started leading Bible studies for women new to the Bible."

Bethany: "When I lead Bible studies, I am always initially scared to death. I am not a speaker, teacher, or leader but a Christ-dedicated organizer. I write everything out in advance, invite other people to help me where I am weak (praying aloud or sharing a faith story). By the end of the study, I am much more comfortable and wish it would never end!"

Sara: "I find that leading a Bible study presses me to make sure I get the Bible study done and do some extra studying. This brings it to the forefront for me to make sure I finish the lessons."

Josie: "I live in a remote area of the state where there are few choices for women's Bible studies. So, I put an invitation on our local Facebook Group page to meet me for a Bible study and waited to see who would respond. Several women wanted to do a Bible study with me. We met together at a local coffee shop."

Janet: "I have mommy friends who need to have some adult discussion. A group of us get together once a week for Bible study right after we drop our children off at school in the morning."

Melanie: "I met with a group of ladies in the evening at a coffee shop one summer while sitting outside under the awning. I met with another group in the café area of the local grocery store over the lunch hour, drawing in women who work from home in our area. Both groups enjoyed the time together."

Connie: "If I don't know the answer to the question asked, I tell them I will find out and let them know the following week. Not having their lessons done annoyed me at one time. Now, I would much rather they came to the study and learned as we discuss the passage and share with one another."

Teresa: "I pray immediately to help manage talkative people, and God always has another intervene for me. I have been inviting a church friend each meeting who has a terrific testimony to talk just before the time I want the ladies to gab. It really helps open them up to feel comfortable to talk."

CHAPTER 11

Use Your Workday Lunch Break for Disciplemaking

JESUS FOLLOWERS BECOME DISCIPLEMAKERS

L unch break. Most people who work during the day take some type of lunch break to satisfy their mid-day hunger and get refreshed for the rest of the workday. What if you spent one of those lunch breaks every week in Bible study with other working women?

I know several women who have gathered coworkers together in their workplace for a weekly women's Bible study over the lunch break. Though the idea sounds inviting, time constraints and experience levels of the women can make this difficult. But with the Lord, nothing is too difficult. He can give you creative ways to use your daily lunch break as a way to fulfill your purpose as a disciplemaker as well. This chapter will explore creative ways to offer a Bible study during your workday lunch break.

Most people who work during the day either from home, in an office, or other workplace environment take some kind of lunch break. These can be great opportunities for doing a Bible study once a week with other women during their workday as well. The time allotted can be short (usually less than an hour). And it might be difficult to find a place. But that is where you can trust Jesus to give you creative ways to use your lunch break for disciplemaking. You can also meet in the evening or other times. But in this chapter, we will be focusing on how to use your workday lunch break for Bible study with other women.

WHERE TO MEET

You have several options for where to meet with other women for a mid-day Bible study—at your job site, at a nearby restaurant or coffee shop, and online.

At the job site as a "Lunch and Learn"

"Lunch and Learn" events are common in most workplaces. What would be the best kind of lunch and learn? The answer to that question would be a Bible study. I know several women who have gathered coworkers together in their workplace for a weekly women's Bible study over the lunch break. They find a room that is unused during lunch and ask their managers for permission to gather there. They bring their own bag lunches, or the group can order something for delivery. Choose easy-to-eat-and-talk food if you do that, nothing complicated.

Is it legal? Yes. There are no legal prohibitions on employers allowing employees, including managers, to conduct voluntary Bible study on their work premises during breaks or outside of working time. You can invite people to join you, but you cannot coerce them to participate in order to gain favor or advancement.

Is it right? Yes. Just make sure to start and stop within the designated time allotted for employees, including you. Being respectful of your employer demonstrates humility and brings honor to the Lord Jesus Christ. This also applies to any one-on-one time you spend talking with another employee. Do it during a break time so that you are not stealing time from your employer. You can view your work as an act of worship, not a curse, and glorify the Lord through your work environment.

At a nearby restaurant

A friend of mine joined with 2 other women from her church who worked in the same area of their city. They invited a few of their coworkers to join them for lunch once a month at a convenient restaurant to their workplaces and said to bring friends. The lunches were short, informal, and good for building relationships—a creative idea for working women who have very little free time to get together with other women. My friend found this to be a great place to invite unchurched coworkers. Something that starts like that can become a Bible study within a few months, perhaps meeting twice a month.

Restaurants and coffee shops can be noisy, making it hard to hear one another. Also, ordering and waiting on food can steal your time to talk. Try to find one that would work well. Some have side rooms you can reserve. If the weather is nice, you can meet outside where it might be quieter.

One summer, I led a Bible study in the café area of a local grocery store over the lunch hour, drawing in women who work from home in our area. We had a little less than an hour to meet, and we did it on Fridays, which was a more relaxed day for most of them. I found out who was interested in joining me then looked for a central location that would work. Everyone either ate at home first or brought their sack lunch to eat while we met. It worked very well for several months.

Through an online app such as Zoom

The use of online apps such as Zoom has opened up a whole new world of meeting together for women. Over the last couple of years, I have been offering a noontime Bible study. Several women who work from home have joined the study. You can do the same with your coworkers, whether you are all working from home or only some of you.

Those are just a few ideas of where to meet. The next question is, "What to study?" From my experience, I suggest you use a short and easy Bible study guide that is designed for anyone new to the Bible.

USE A SHORT AND EASY BIBLE STUDY GUIDE

Most published women's studies involve too much homework for the average working woman to be able to do at home with her restricted time. And any accompanying videos are just too long to leave any room in the weekly gathering for discussion and getting to know one another. At best, a workplace lunch break allows for 45 minutes of actual discussion time.

Besides the time constraint for a lunchtime Bible study with coworkers, there is also the wide variety of Bible knowledge background or lack of knowledge that each woman brings to the group. And you want to get everyone into the Bible for themselves. That means choosing a Bible study not a popular book that has a few Bible verses in it. [You can go to my website and download the "Start and Lead a Bible Study Group" booklet for help in choosing a Bible study for your group.]

The best solution is a Bible study that is short and easy for anyone to understand. You want something short enough to be done together during that lunch hour and asking them to do less than an hour's worth of reading and reflecting on some Bible passages at home.

Over the past years as I have gone to many churches to train women for disciplemaking in their personal lives, I have seen the need for Bible studies designed especially for anyone new to the Bible. So many adult women these days have never learned to read or study the Bible for themselves. When they try one of our typical studies, women who are new to the Bible feel lost and ignorant because most studies assume previous Bible knowledge. It can be very discouraging. We covered this in Chapter 8.

Our ministry now offers several beginners' Bible studies that are perfect for one-on-one discipling of new Christians and can be done during the typical lunch break at work. The series of books is called *Graceful Beginnings*. Each book contains Bible lessons that are basic, easy to understand, using simple terms, and very relationship-with-God oriented. Currently there are eight available on my website and through most online bookstores. You can freely download each of these studies to check them out. These are the ones I use during the online studies I lead during the lunch hour.

What we have to offer

❖ *A Fresh Start*: This one covers the first steps towards a new life in Christ. Basic foundational truths about who Jesus is, who God is, who the Holy Spirit is, and how to live in this new relationship with God.

❖ *Painting the Portrait of Jesus*: This one covers the self-portrait of Jesus using His seven "I am" statements in the gospel of John. Get to know who He is and why He is someone we want to follow.

❖ *The God You Can Know*: This is a quick look into the attributes of our Father God and why His love can be trusted.

❖ *Grace Overflowing:* See how Christ is revealed in Paul's letters and how we can live in His grace daily.

❖ *The Walk from Fear to Faith*: Learn to trust God with your fears as you look at the lives of Old Testament Women.

❖ *Satisfied by His Love:* Learn how to let Jesus satisfy your heart with the goodness of His love as you look at His interaction with several New Testament Women.

❖ *Seek the Treasure*: This is a simple study of the book of Ephesians.

❖ *Pathways to a Joyful Walk:* Learn some foundational truths so that you will have a rewarding spiritual life.

STAY CHRIST-FOCUSED & TAKE THE NEXT STEPS

For anyone reading this chapter who works in an environment with other women, please try a lunchtime Bible study. Doing so is part of lifestyle disciplemaking. In fact, inviting coworkers to CONNECT with them leads to studying the Bible to ESTABLISH them in truth. And that LAUNCHES you into ministry beyond your church setting. It is a win/win!

Disciplemaking is the Lord Jesus Christ's idea and commission to all of His followers. What He calls us to do, He enables us to do through His Spirit at work in us and in the world. Trust Him to show you what to do to offer a Bible study to coworkers during your lunch break. Then, watch what He does!

Our last chapter is addressed to anyone leading a ministry at church, especially women's ministry. We will discuss how to transition an existing ministry to one that is more disciple-making focused.

Let Jesus lead you into lifestyle disciplemaking.
Jesus followers become disciplemakers.

TAKE THE LEAP

Thought questions

1. What are your hesitations about asking coworkers to join you in a Bible study? Give these over to the Lord and trust Him to help you.

2. Do you already know of other Christians in your workplace? How could you bring them into the planning for a lunch break Bible study once a week or so?

Action steps for individuals

1. Consider how you can offer a Bible study to your coworkers. Consider the suggestions above and ask the Lord to show you what you could do. Ask a Christian friend to join you in prayer regarding this.

2. Find some women who work in the same area of town where you work who might partner with you in doing a lunch hour group at

a nearby restaurant or gathering place. This would give you someone to share the inviting and leading.

Action steps for ministry leaders

1. Pray about how you can best encourage women in the workforce to be disciplemakers in their work environment. Then, look at all the suggestions we have made in this book about resources and preparation they might need. Make sure you have those readily available. Frequently promote this way of launching disciplemakers.

2. Challenge women in the workforce to start and lead Bible studies for their coworkers. Pray for the Lord to give them a desire to do this. Provide leader training for them and suggested resources to use. Give them support as needed.

Prayer prompts

✓ Ask Jesus to give you the courage and drive to start and lead a Bible study for your female coworkers.

✓ Trust Him to help you each step of the way including to give you favor with your employer if you would like to meet onsite. Watch what the Lord does through this!

What others have done

Yvonne: "I had the idea of finding other women from my church who work in the same area of the city as I do. I found a few, invited them to join me for lunch once a month at a convenient restaurant to their workplaces, and said to bring friends. The lunches are short, informal, and good for building relationships—a creative idea for working women who have very little free time to get together with other women. I found this to be a great place to invite unchurched coworkers."

Hayley: "I invited some coworkers to join me during the lunch break. I asked for permission to use a conference room. Several of us met for eight weeks. We discovered that this built some community among employees who had not previously known about each other's faith."

CHAPTER 12

Transition to a Disciplemaking-Focused Women's Ministry

JESUS FOLLOWERS BECOME DISCIPLEMAKERS

H as your ministry team been event-driven with one person overseeing Bible studies, another the retreat, & another the Christmas brunch? Does your current women's ministry need to have more structure and purpose to what you organize and fund? Do you see the same women involved in your ministry with rarely a new face? Do you recognize Jesus' leading for you to have a greater focus on disciplemaking for the women of your church? If you answered yes to any (or all) of those questions, now is the time to transition your women's ministry from being event-driven to disciplemaking-focused! You will learn how to do that in this chapter.

WHAT IS EFFECTIVE MINISTRY?

How do you determine your ministry effectiveness? Do you have any specific criteria based on biblical guidelines?

I read this quote more than ten years ago when I was traveling from church to church training women for disciplemaking. It still resonates with me.

> An effective ministry is not necessarily a big or busy ministry, but one that is **regularly reaching new people for Christ**, building them up in the faith and equipping them to reach their generation for Christ." (Sonlife Ministries, *Growing Healthy Women in Ministry*, page 18)

Big and busy. That is what happens to any growing ministry segment of a church. The more people coming into the church community, the more programs are added to accommodate them. The problem is that programs without real purpose related to all aspects of disciplemaking are missing the mark.

The terms "discipleship" and "disciplemaking" often get confused. Most churches I have attended have been heavily focused on discipleship. As I mentioned before, discipleship typically refers to the normal process for Christians to grow in their faith through Bible studies, prayer, worship, and small groups. It usually focuses on individual spiritual growth. Discipleship is an essential part of getting established in your faith. But it is only one-third of what Jesus commissioned us to do.

THREE PHASES OF EFFECTIVE MINISTRY

The quote above outlines the three phases of the disciplemaking process:

- **Regularly reaching new people** for Christ (the CONNECT phase)
- **Building them up** in the faith (the ESTABLISH phase)
- **Training and releasing them to reach** their generation for Christ (the LAUNCH phase)

Disciplemaking includes seeing people trust in Christ and grow in their faith. It also includes training Christians to reach new people for Christ and help new believers grow in their faith so those can then reach their own peers for Christ.

Women of all ages and stages of life can learn to share their faith and disciple new believers. Wherever women gather, disciplemaking can take place there. Leaders in women's ministry need to keep all aspects of disciplemaking in mind as they plan activities for the year.

Disciplemaking makes disciples who make more disciples. It is others-focused more than self-focused. Focused is a key concept in a disciplemaking ministry. Where is your focus?

Clarify "women's ministry"

We need to define what we mean by "women's ministry" in this chapter. Many church ministries involve women in teaching children's classes, serving in local missions, and being on the worship team. Those are not considered "women's ministry." Women's ministry is whatever is offered **to** women and **for** women so each one can know and live out her commissioned two-fold purpose: 1) to follow Jesus as His disciple and 2) to live for Jesus as a disciplemaker.

LOSING A DISCIPLEMAKING FOCUS

I asked several questions at the beginning of this chapter.

❖ *Has your ministry team been event-driven with one person overseeing Bible studies, another the retreat, & another the Christmas brunch?* This is how most women's leadership teams are organized. Event-driven. Not disciplemaking-driven.

❖ *Does your current women's ministry need to have more structure and purpose to what you organize and fund?* Often, you do what the women want to do. If you leave planning up to what women want, the result will be lots of fellowship activities with other Christians, and some Bible studies thrown in for developing close friends. Nothing is wrong with having fun together. But Jesus commissioned us to make disciples who make disciples. That begins at the local church and spreads out to those who need Christ. It will not always be comfortable.

❖ *Do you see the same women involved in your ministry with rarely a new face?* I was in a church once that was quite exclusive. Only those who had the same values as the leading families were invited to participate in anything. It was closed to nonbelievers and even getting trained to reach out to nonbelievers. I was rather shocked!

If you answered yes to any (or all) of those questions I asked, you have strayed from Jesus' commission to every Christian to become a disciplemaker. This is a challenge in all churches. We get comfortable with doing things a certain way and can lose perspective. Now is the time to transition your women's ministry to a disciplemaking-focused one!

TRANSITION TO A DISCIPLEMAKING-FOCUSED MINISTRY

Start with prayer. Ask Jesus to show you the weak areas in your women's ministry regarding disciplemaking. Ask Him for courage to change some events or activities to encourage disciplemaking. Trust Him to help you see a better way for utilizing your church resources and people to advance everyone into lifestyle disciplemaking. Then, proceed through the following steps.

There is a 6-step strategy to transition your women's ministry from event-driven to disciplemaking-focused. You can go to my website and download the "Transition to a Disciplemaking-Focused

Women's Ministry" booklet. It contains the following steps plus a chart that will help you list and evaluate existing ministries.

Step 1: EVALUATE existing ministries for their disciplemaking purpose

To evaluate existing ministries for purpose and effectiveness in disciplemaking, first list the activities you offer to women, whether ongoing (weekly/monthly) or occasional (once a year).

Consider the primary purpose of each activity and whether you can place that activity under one of these categories: CONNECT (reaches nonbelievers or prepares women to reach nonbelievers), ESTABLISH (grows women to establish strong roots as believers whether long-time or new), or LAUNCH (launches women in their communities to reach their peers for Christ and prepares new leaders to establish believers both inside and outside of the church). If you are unsure about an activity's purpose, mark it as "Unclear Disciplemaking Purpose."

Step 2: ENHANCE existing activities for disciplemaking

Explore ways to enhance existing activities to make them more effective for disciplemaking. This might include:

CONNECT:

- Making some ministries more receptive for new people, including childcare spots for the unchurched.
- Designing the activity more for the community and promote it invitingly.
- Recruiting and preparing designated engagers for specific activities, including follow-up. See Chapter 3.

ESTABLISH:

- Adding a group for beginners to your existing Bible studies. See Chapter 8.
- Offering a variety of study levels that are also cross-generational.
- Training your small group leaders for disciplemaking in their groups. See Chapter 7.

LAUNCH:

- Train and encourage women to connect with nonbelievers, practice telling their faith stories, and practice sharing the gospel message. See Chapters 2-5.

- Give training and encouragement to women to start and lead Bible studies outside of church ministries. See Chapter 10.

Step 3: REPLACE those activities less effective for disciplemaking

Consider how to change or stop and replace those activities that do not have a disciplemaking purpose or have become less effective. Be willing to "blow things up" to encourage disciplemaking.

In her book, *Community Is Messy*, Heather Zempel wrote a whole chapter on being willing to "blow things up" when an activity or event is no longer effective at doing what it is supposed to accomplish. She calls it "Operation Kaboom" and says that it requires humility and honesty to recognize that what worked yesterday may not work today—or may never have worked at all!

She gives this advice for the process of "blowing things up" to change or replace a favorite activity:

> Be humble, be prayerful, be discerning. ... Make sure God has initiated the process, and invite Him to be a part of it all the way through. ... Be willing to hurt some feelings and offend some people. ... Stop doing things that are really good to make way for things that are better. Just because you've 'always done it that way' doesn't mean you should keep doing it that way. (Heather Zempel, *Community Is Messy*, page 168)

This is hard to do. Women do not like change. We get attached and even possessive about ministries we have started or have held together for years. This can cause an angry backlash.

Heather Zempel recognizes this and takes us back to focus on our purpose.

> There may be some [activities] that you really love, that carry sentimental value for many people and that even accomplish good things. But they are no longer the right thing. Be willing to [stop] good things to make way for

better things. (Heather Zempel, *Community Is Messy*, page 168)

When we are truly open to the Lord's leading, we must be willing to let go of our cherished way of doing things if they are not successfully leading new people to Jesus, establishing new believers well, and launching everyone into lifestyle disciplemaking. A few tweaks may not fix it. Time to "kaboom!"

Let me insert a caution here. Move slowly with your "Operation Kaboom." Consider whether that activity can be moved to another church ministry (local missions or hospitality or assimilation) or released to an individual to continue doing it apart from women's ministry. Always plan a time of celebration and appreciation whenever you end it.

Step 4: CONSIDER new ways to address the weak areas

First, you have to consider the weak areas from your evaluation above. But I have recognized three general weak areas in a typical women's ministry:

- ❖ The **lack of preparedness** to befriend and share one's faith with unchurched women. We have discussed that throughout this book.

- ❖ The **disconnected** women. Who is left out of your current ministry? Why? Where can you draw them into the community of women so they can grow and be encouraged to reach their peers for Christ? What if they work nights and weekends? Can you offer a variety of times to include them?

- ❖ The **immediate neighbors**. How do you reach the women in the neighborhoods closest to your church? My daughter attended a church that intentionally reached out to the people in the houses and apartments immediately surrounding the church building. Twice a year, the whole congregation went "visiting" in that neighborhood after some preparation taught during the church service.

What do you recognize as the weak areas in your women's ministry regarding disciplemaking?

Step 5: TRANSFORM the team to the disciplemaking mission

My husband often uses this phrase, **"Match the team to the mission."** He uses it in a business context, but it applies very well in a ministry context. What would that look like in women's ministry to match the team to the mission?

Match the leadership team members to the process of disciplemaking (Connect, Establish, and Launch) to help you stay balanced in the areas of disciplemaking. By transforming your leadership team to the disciplemaking mission, you can help the women of your church move away from dependence on traditional event-driven ministries and toward a lifestyle of making disciples who make more disciples. The local church is the best venue for disciplemaking to begin.

Transforming your women's ministry to the disciplemaking mission will help you as a ministry **move beyond event-driven leadership**. Here is how to do that:

1. **Match** the leadership team members to one of three aspects of disciplemaking (Connect, Establish, or Launch) as a way of staying balanced. Ask Jesus to draw each team member to one of those three aspects of disciplemaking.

2. **Determine** how you will respond when others come to you with a ministry idea. Ask the questions below while praying for guidance:

   - What would be the main purpose of this ministry—to Connect, Establish, or Launch?

   - Will this ministry activity reach nonbelievers? Will it produce new disciples? Support and fund what will lead to new disciples and disciplemakers.

You can download our "Transition to a Disciplemaking-Focused Women's Ministry" booklet. It contains suggestions to help you transform your ministry team to become more disciplemaking-focused.

Step 6: RECRUIT a Disciplemaking Coach to support discipling relationships

Recruit a "Disciplemaking Coach" to support women in one-to-one discipling relationships and to assist your leadership team in staying focused on your disciplemaking purpose. Ask Jesus to bring someone's name to mind you could ask—someone who has experience and a passion for lifestyle disciplemaking. Invite her to become a disciplemaking coach for women in your church.

This is what she might do as part of her coaching ministry:

- Advise the women's ministry team during planning sessions in determining whether existing activities or new ones being considered have any disciplemaking purpose.

- Oversee the designated engagers for activities open to visitors. See Chapter 3.

- Support and encourage women who are discipling others. Remind them to stay dependent on the Holy Spirit as they are pursuing lifestyle disciplemaking.

- Supply transferable one-to-one discipling resources. Know where they are. Resupply as needed. See Chapter 7.

STAY CHRIST-FOCUSED & TAKE THE NEXT STEPS

Remember the purpose of making the transition to a disciplemaking-focused ministry is to prepare and encourage every Christian woman to pursue lifestyle disciplemaking in her daily walk with the Lord. That fulfills our commissioned purpose to follow Jesus as His disciple and to live for Him as a disciplemaker throughout our lives.

Disciplemaking is the Lord Jesus Christ's idea and commission to all of His followers. What He calls us to do, He enables us to do through His Spirit at work in us and in the world. Trust Him to show you what to do as you transition your women's ministry from being event-driven to disciplemaking-focused. Then, watch what He does!

Let Jesus lead you into lifestyle disciplemaking.
Jesus followers become disciplemakers.

TAKE THE LEAP

Thought questions

1. What do you recognize as the weak areas in your ministry regarding disciplemaking?

2. Who are those who may currently feel left out of existing church ministries? Why are they left out?

3. What is your usual focus as you plan your ministry activities? Do you remember the goal is not just to produce disciples of Jesus but to grow disciplemakers for Jesus? Why or why not?

4. Are you personally willing to dissolve or change favorite activities and events that are not effective at disciplemaking? If not, why not?

Action steps for individuals

1. Talk to your ministry leaders about disciplemaking and becoming more focused on disciplemaking in their ministry planning and outreach.

2. Volunteer to be a disciplemaking coach to anyone who is connecting with their nonbelieving peers and / or discipling a new believer. Keep your ministry leaders informed about successes and challenges.

Action steps for ministry leaders

1. Work through the "Transition to a Disciplemaking-Focused Women's Ministry" strategy to evaluate existing ministries for effectiveness at disciplemaking. You can download the booklet for this from melanienewton.com/disciplemaking. It also contains a chart we have developed to help you list and evaluate existing ministries

2. Be willing to change or replace some events or activities to encourage disciplemaking.

3. Look for creative ways to include those who may currently feel left out of existing church ministries so that you can both reach them and train them to reach their peers.

4. If you need help with this transition, invite Melanie Newton to come to your church and lead your ministry team through this "Transition to a Disciplemaking-Focused Women's Ministry" strategy. We will work through each of the above 6 steps together to help you make your women's ministry more lifestyle disciplemaking-focused.

5. Read the blog, *Stop the 'It's MY Ministry' Mentality,* on Bible.org to see what happened at two churches when trying to change or replace existing ministries and the challenges that resulted.

Prayer prompts

- ✓ Ask Jesus to show you the weak areas in your women's ministry regarding disciplemaking.

- ✓ Ask Him for humility and courage to change some events or activities to encourage disciplemaking.

- ✓ Trust Him to help you see a better way for using your church resources and people to advance everyone into lifestyle disciplemaking.

What others have done

Jennie: "God has been moving in the hearts of women to refresh our women's ministry. Since the women of our church have a long history of linking arms to serve the church and the community, we want to carry forth that heart as we train all women to be disciplemakers by living, sharing, and showing the Gospel. Our newly restructured women's ministry team will be evaluating our current ministry to women and charting a course so that our women's ministry connects, establishes, and launches as we grow as disciplemakers together."

Melanie: "My daughter attended a church that intentionally reached out to the people in the houses and apartments immediately surrounding the church building. Twice a year, the whole congregation went "visiting" in that neighborhood after some preparation taught during the church service."

Keith: "We were blessed by the Lifestyle Disciplemaking workshop at our church. About a month after the event our women had a Faith Story party to practice sharing their stories. For many, it was the first time they learned to share their faith. Our women's Bible study intentionally built in a new focus on multiplying leaders. They began intentionally inviting women outside the church. They also started to invite millennial-aged young women and have small group break out with them at the women's study. One of our gals was so inspired she started meeting with two college girls God placed on her heart. The workshop also caused our women in leadership roles to step back and honestly evaluate the overall picture of our women's ministry. It created conversations that are helping us to move toward more of an emphasis on reaching those who do not know Jesus and multiplying healthy disciples."

Lifestyle Disciplemaking Resources

We have many lifestyle disciplemaking resources on my website melanienewton.com (including everything offered in this book).

"Disciplemaking" page

❖ "Pray and Love" bookmark

❖ "Designated Engagers Preparation" checklist

❖ "Prepare to Share" booklet

❖ "Establish a New or Young Christian" booklet

❖ "Start and Lead a Bible Study Group" booklet

❖ "Transition to a Disciplemaking-Focused Women's Ministry" booklet

❖ *Be a Christ-Focused Small Group Leader* (handbook for leaders that includes a chapter on disciplemaking in your small group)

❖ Links to resources for new believers from other trusted websites

❖ "Leap into Lifestyle Disciplemaking Retreat"

"Bible Studies" page

❖ *Live Out His Love Bible Study* (a study of New Testament women, with disciplemaking applications)

❖ *A Fresh Start Bible Study* (for new Christians)

❖ *Graceful Beginnings Bible Studies* (short and easy, good for anyone new to the Bible)

"Blogs" page

❖ *Lifestyle Disciplemaking* series of blogs

❖ *Counter the "Work Is Secular" Infection* blog

❖ *The Gospel: God's Cure for Our Sin Disease* series of blogs

❖ *Live a Question-Stimulating Life in View of Your Neighbor*s on Bible.org

❖ *Stop the 'It's MY Ministry' Mentality* on Bible.org to see how to change or replace existing ministries and the challenges that resulted at two churches

"Podcasts" page

❖ Series 17 podcasts *"Disciplemaking"*

References

1. Barry D. Jones, *Dwell: Life with God for the World*
2. Chuck Swindoll quote
3. David Souther, EvanTell.org
4. Dwight L. Moody quote
5. Evantell.org website
6. Heather Zempel, Community Is Messy
7. Jill Briscoe quote
8. Joe Aldrich, *Lifestyle Evangelism*
9. Major Ian Thomas, *The Saving Life of Christ*
10. Neal and Judy Brower, *Pray and Watch*
11. ResoundNow, *Disciplemaking Pathway Training Guide*
12. ResoundNow, *The Disciplemaking Ministry Guide for Women in Leadership*
13. Sonlife Ministries, *Growing Healthy Women in Ministry*
14. *The Evangelism Study Bible*